ONE GOD,
MANY WORLDS

ONE GOD,
MANY WORLDS

Teachings of a Renewed Hasidism

A Festschrift in Honor of
Rabbi Zalman Schachter-Shalomi, z"l

Edited by
Netanel Miles-Yépez

Foreword by
Nehemia Polen

Albion
Andalus
Boulder, Colorado
2015

"The old shall be renewed,
and the new shall be made holy."
— Rabbi Avraham Yitzhak Kook

One God, Many Worlds: Teachings of a Renewed Hasidism: A Festschrift in Honor of Rabbi Zalman Schachter-Shalomi, z"l
© 2015 Netanel Miles-Yépez

Albion-Andalus, Inc.
P. O. Box 19852
Boulder, CO 80308
www.albionandalus.com

Design and layout by Albion-Andalus Books
Cover design by Sari Wisenthal-Shore
Cover photo of Rabbi Zalman Schachter in Winnipeg, Canada, ca. 1974.
Pen and Ink illustrations of "Rabbi Zalman Schachter" and Rabbi Yosef Yitzhak Schneersohn" by Netanel Miles-Yépez.

ISBN-13: 978-0692499016 (Albion-Andalus Books)
ISBN-10: 0692499016

For Reb Zalman
May his memory be a blessing

Contents

Acknowledgments   ix
Preface   xi
Foreword by *Nehemia Polen*   xiii

The Teachings of
Yosef Yitzhak Schneersohn of Lubavitch

A Call for a Renewed Ḥavurah   3
Arthur Green

A Letter on Meditation   11
Miles Krassen

Contemplation in Prayer   21
Ruth Gan Kagan

Wisdom from the Habad Lineage   25
Laura Duhan Kaplan

The Rabbi Turned Coachman   33
Rami Shapiro

A Table in the Presence of My Enemies   51
Neal Rose

One God, Many Worlds   65
Netanel Miles-Yepez

The Bridal Chamber   85
Tirzah Firestone

The Teachings of
Menachem Mendel Schneerson of Lubavitch

When Will the Wedding Take Place?   95
Shaul Magid

Going Home Again   107
Emanuel Goldmann

Searchin'   111
  Matisyahu Miller
Teaching Torah   117
  Bahir Davis

THE TEACHINGS OF
SHLOMO HALBERSTAM OF BOBOV

Trees, Vineyards, and the Master Gardener   125
  Thomas Atum O'Kane
How Will God Bring Us Back to Zion?   131
  Michael L. Kagan
The Healing Question   143
  Lynn Gottlieb

THE TEACHINGS OF
GEDALIAH KENIG OF S'FAT

You Have the Da'at You Need   153
  Shalvi Schachter Waldman

APPENDICES

Notes for a Lecture by the Late Lubavitcher Rebbe 161
Geologist of the Soul   167
A Poetic Remembering by Carol Rose   169

Contributor Biographies   171

ACKNOWLEDGMENTS

I WISH TO THANK all the contributors: Rabbi Bahir Davis, Rabbi Tirzah Firestone, Pastor Emanuel Goldmann, Rabbi Lynn Gottlieb, Rabbi Dr. Arthur Green, Maggid Michael Kagan, Rabbi Ruth Gan Kagan, Rabbi Laura Duhan Kaplan, Rabbi Miles Krassen, Rabbi Dr. Shaul Magid, Matisyahu Miller, Thomas Atum O'Kane, Rabbi Dr. Nehemia Polen, Carol Rose, Rabbi Dr. Neal Rose, Rabbi Rami Shapiro, and Shalvi Schachter Waldman. I also wish to thank the following people: Pir Zia Inayat-Khan, for honoring Reb Zalman on his *yahrzeit;* my inimitable friend, Jennifer Alia Wittman, for use of the Abode of the Message library in New Lebanon, New York; Waduda Welch and Noor Amina for hosting my talk on the Four Worlds in Boulder, Colorado; Hallaj Michalenko of the Front Range Sufi Order for hosting my talk on the Four Worlds in Denver, Colorado; my friend, Rabbi Zvi Ish-Shalom, who I consulted on a point or two; Stella Bonnie and Lasette Brown, who worked alongside me in various coffee shops and at dining room tables in Boulder; and Eve Ilsen, my kind and loving friend, who hosted me as I put the finishing touches on this volume.

— N.M-Y.

PREFACE

IN 2004, AS A GIFT for my *rebbe* Rabbi Zalman Schachter-Shalomi's 80th birthday, I decided to invite a number of his students and colleagues to contribute to a *festschrift* or commemorative volume in his honor. To make the volume truly unique, I asked each contributor to update or give a new presentation to teachings by Reb Zalman's own rebbes which he had himself translated into English, or to stories that he had told of them. These included teachings and stories of Rabbi Yosef Yitzhak Schneersohn of Lubavitch (1880-1950), Rabbi Menachem Mendel Schneerson of Lubavitch (1902-1994), and Rabbi Shlomo Halberstam of Bobov (1908-2000). The idea was to see how these same teachings might be presented today, according to the paradigm-shifted understanding of Reb Zalman's own colleagues, close collaborators, and students. As editor, I chose pieces that I felt would suit or challenge particular contributors and asked them to approach each creatively and with fresh eyes.

That original *festschrift* was comprised of fourteen contributions, including: a dedicatory poem by Carol Rose, an appreciation by Rabbi Dr. Nehemia Polen, and contributions by Rabbi Bahir Davis, Rabbi Tirzah Firestone, Pastor Emanuel Goldmann, Rabbi Lynn Gottlieb, Rabbi Dr. Arthur Green, Maggid Michael and Rabbi Ruth Gan Kagan, Rabbi Laura Duhan Kaplan, Rabbi Miles Krassen, Rabbi Dr. Shaul Magid, Thomas Atum O'Kane, Rabbi Or-Nistar Rose, Rabbi Dr. Neal Rose, and Rabbi Rami Shapiro. A single bound copy was made for Reb Zalman and presented personally to him on his birthday, August 17th, 2004. One year later, in September of 2005, each contribution was posted in the first issue of the on-line journal, *Spectrum: A Journal of Renewal Spirituality.*

In 2014, as Reb Zalman's 90th birthday approached, it seemed a good time to update the collection and to publish it formally. The previous contributors reviewed and corrected their contributions and new contributions were solicited. These included pieces by the recording artist, Matisyahu, a talmudic reflection from Michael Kagan, a teaching on the Four Worlds by myself, and a new teaching from Reb Zalman's daughter, Shalvi Schachter Waldman, taking off from a story Reb Zalman told of his Bratzlaver friend, Gedaliah Kenig.

Sadly, Reb Zalman passed away on July 3rd, 2014, roughly a month and a half shy of his 90th birthday. Though he had been ill for some time, his passing nevertheless came as a shock to many of us. Needless to say, the *festschrift* was put on hold. Everyone who had contributed was committed to its eventual completion, but it would take a year before the last contributions were finished and assembled. Now, just weeks after his first *yahrzeit,* and approximately a month before what would have been his 91st birthday, the volume is complete. It is hoped that its teachings will be of benefit to the many admirers of Hasidic spirituality who are committed to its continuance, and that it will be seen as an extension of Reb Zalman's own profound legacy.

Netanel Miles-Yépez
Louisville, Kentucky, August 17th, 2015
Reb Zalman's 91st birthday

FOREWORD

Rabbi Dr. Nehemia Polen

THE YEAR WAS 1978. I had just started a doctoral program at Boston University with Elie Wiesel and was looking for a dissertation topic relating to the areas of Hasidism and the Holocaust. During a discussion at Havurat Shalom in Somerville, Massachusetts, I asked Rabbi Zalman Schachter if he had any ideas for me. He immediately suggested the Piasetzner Rebbe and his *Aish Kodesh*. At the time, the master and his work were not well known; there was almost nothing written on him in English. Nevertheless, Reb Zalman knew the *Aish Kodesh* quite well. What impresses me now, thirty-six years and much work later, as I recall our initial conversation, is that Reb Zalman got it: he grasped the *Aish Kodesh*'s historical and theological significance; its spiritual and emotional power; and the light it shed on the Piasetzner and his greatness. The major themes I was to uncover, the soaring spiritual trajectory emerging in dramatic contrast to the relentless unfolding of catastrophe; the defiance and triumph of the soul—Reb Zalman saw them all and pointed the way for me at the very beginning.

A similar story can be told in many other related domains of Jewish life and creative encounter with tradition: *davvenen* as spiritual practice; the Four Worlds as a usable roadmap of the cosmos; fruitful engagement with the variety of humanity's great religious personalities and traditions; and so on. Many of his pioneering insights have now been adapted and adopted in the mainstream as the shared language of Jewish religious expression in our time. And whatever he gave, he gave *be-ayin yafeh*, with a 'good eye,' with a spirit of generosity and blessing, with no expectation other than the blessing be shared further—which it has. Reb Zalman saw it all and pointed the way from the beginning. He was blessed to live to see the flowering of much of his noble and far-reaching vision, and we who have benefitted from it, are eternally grateful and in his debt.

THE TEACHINGS OF
YOSEF YITZHAK SCHNEERSOHN
OF LUBAVITCH

A CALL FOR A RENEWED HAVURAH

RABBI ARTHUR GREEN

This teaching is based on notes made in preparation for a talk by the sixth Lubavitcher Rebbe, Rabbi Yosef Yitzhak Schneersohn. Believing these notes to be of particular significance, Reb Zalman translated and published them as "Notes for a Lecture by the Late Lubavitcher Rebbe" (see Appendices).[1] Here, Arthur Green, one of the world's foremost interpreters of Hasidism and a longtime friend and colleague of Reb Zalman, re-presents the Rebbe's message in contemporary terms.

— N.M-Y., editor

MY FRIENDS AND STUDENTS:

We are engaged in a great and awesome struggle for the soul of Torah.

Torah, meaning 'instruction' or 'direction' has existed within the Jewish people for several thousand years, passed on faithfully from one generation to the next. As it was passed on, each generation added to it of its own spirit, reshaping it in accord with the needs of the hour and the inner voices it heard to guide it. The process begins with Moshe, as the talmudic tractate 'Principles' (Avot) says in its opening line, "Moshe received Torah from Sinai and passed it [lit. 'her'] to Yehoshua." Note that it does not say, "Moshe received the Torah from Sinai," but "Torah." Torah is not merely a text or a fixed body of teachings,

---

1 Zalman Schachter-Shalomi, "Notes for a Lecture by the Late Lubavitcher Rebbe," *Four Worlds Journal* (Vol. 3, No. 2: Fall, 1986/5747), 11-17.

something to which the definite article could be applied. Torah is the process of instruction, the moment of communication between master and disciple, student and fellow-learner. That communication involves the opening of heart and mind, those of both the 'giver' and the 'receiver' in a moment of teaching. The receiver will then become a giver in the next moment as the teaching is carried farther, enriched and subtly transformed by the voice and soul of its latest bearer. Torah is that entire process, from Moshe and Yehoshua to the very moment in which I write and you read these words, and far, far beyond.

Our struggle begins with an awareness of this process. So many of those who think they love Torah most, who are seen by themselves and the world as Torah's most faithful servants (of whom it is said, "Look how religious they are, since they follow the commandments so strictly"), understand little if anything of what the transmission process is all about. Their mission is to keep Torah just as it was back in Volozhyn, or Satmar, or Lubavitch for that matter, unchanged in any way. Even if they dress in fine Hasidic garb, they are *mitnagedim* at heart, because they fail to understand the great liberating message of the holy Ba'al Shem Tov and his disciples. Torah should not be a heavy burden, they taught, weighing you down with obsessive-ness and guilt ("Did I do it right? Did I fulfill my obligation?"). Rather, it should make you lighter, more able to leap upward, to reach toward heaven. That is what the Rabbis meant when they said about the Holy Ark: *Ha-aron nose' et nose'av:* "The ark carries those who carry it!" Being a bearer of Torah should fill you with lightness and joy, as though you are being carried on the wings of cherubim.

To keep Torah light in this way, it has to be reinterpreted *by* and *for* each generation. "Torah is eternal," the Hasidic commentaries repeat week after week, "so what does this verse have to say to us?" How can we open it up (as in *"Rabbi Shim'on patah"*) so that it can take us, our very unique generation of questioners and seekers, into it, making us a part of the process? Only when that happens, when Torah becomes open to us, can we turn to our own disciples and urge them—"Open your hearts to Torah." This was the secret of the Hasidic masters: they reshaped Torah to make room for their generations of Jews, and they reshaped those Jews to make room in their hearts for this ever-expanding, ever-renewing Torah.

Hasidism did this predominately through multi-leveled truth. The Rabbis' notion that "Torah has seventy faces" was their way of saying that you can keep going on, endlessly, re-reading the same verse, word or letter, as the new soul-energy of unique human minds and hearts are applied to it. When the Midrash offers multiple readings of a text, introducing each one with *"davar aher* [another matter; another reading]," it reminds us that all these readings, and many more, are equally valid, equally true, each of them refracting the soul-prisms of the one who spoke it.

In the later tradition, these infinitely varied readings mostly take on the name of *nistar*, 'hidden' meanings, using the interpretive tools of *kabbalah* to expand and deepen the meanings to be found within the text and within the person. As the Zohar so powerfully teaches, the surface meaning of the Torah text is only the apparent meaning of Torah, not its deep truth. 'Apparent' as is 'apparel'— the outer meaning is the garment of Torah. Our task is to undress the bride (or groom, for that matter), to go on first to the body, then to the soul, and ultimately to the still unknowable 'soul of soul' within Torah. We embark on this journey with tools given us by tradition: good Hebrew, knowledge of past interpretations, and fluency with kabbalistic symbols are all a great help. But we also cannot embark without the opening of heart and mind.

The struggle for the soul of Torah is against those who would deny this ongoing process of rebirth and transformation in the very midst of affirming Torah. Some of those are the literalists, those who seek to read Torah as a true historical record of events as they 'really" happened, of actual persons, places, and times. They don't want us to go 'into' the text, but rather to stay on its surface, professing our loyalty to the fact that there really was a man named Lavan, that he really had two daughters, that he really cheated our ancestor Ya'akov, and all the rest. They have forsaken the richness of the Rabbis' free and poly-vocal reading of Torah, bringing a new and alien fundamentalism into Jewish life. Although borne by bearers of black hats and *sheytelekh,* carried into the classrooms of day schools throughout the Jewish world, this doggedly literalist reading (sometimes including RaSHI as well as the text!) lacks the richness, lightness, and sense of humor required to give it a real *Yidishn tam,* an authentic Jewish flavor.

A second group of deniers, who would be surprised, even shocked to be grouped alongside the first, are the critical scholars. These too insist that *peshat* is the only Torah, that the text is uni-dimensional and can only be understood properly in the Ancient Near Eastern context, its most strange and inviting words to be interpreted exclusively through the Ugaritic cognates. All the rest, as far as they are concerned, is nonsense. "*Mere* homiletics," they insist, "not scholarship." But the point, of course, is homiletics, if you need to call it that. "Our rebbe," says the Lubavitcher Ḥasid, "teaches Torah that carries you to the highest heavens!" "Our Rebbe," replies the Kotzker, "says Torah that hits you right here in the gut." How do they do this? Homiletics, of course; keeping Torah alive and powerful for each generation. Based in the text, reading the sources, but bringing them yet again to real life. That's what it's all about.

But the greatest battle, sometimes including and sometimes reaching beyond both of the above, has to do with narrowness of mind. "Small-mindedness," said my Rebbe, Abraham Joshua Heschel, "causes exile of the *Shekhinah* [the divine presence]." Small-mindedness, in our case, means commitment to *the* Torah, the identification of 'Torah' with 'Judaism' and the smug self-assurance that it exists only among Jews. In its most extreme forms, this manifests in a belief in Jewish spiritual superiority and exclusiveness in religious truth-claims. It says that God chose the Jews not to be "a kingdom of priests," ministering to all of humanity (for what is a priest without a congregation?), but rather to be the unique bearers of truth through history, closed off to the world, required to give nothing to others, until God sends our very Jewish Messiah.

The Rabbis were deeply aware of this danger; they saw it growing in their own midst. They therefore offered teachings to subtly undermine such claims, but those teachings need to be understood properly. Judaism was for centuries the tradition of an oppressed minority, who were told loudly and repeatedly that ours was a vanquished and useless heritage. Therefore, the Rabbis had to couch their universalist teachings in carefully guarded phrases, so as not to undermine the need a weakened Jewish body politic had for defenses against attack. When the Rabbis taught that Avraham our Father fulfilled the entire Torah before it was given, they were opening the doorway for us. Avraham's children of course include Christians and Muslims, not just Jews. Torah, in the fullest sense, is thus potentially accessible to all his heirs. Avraham himself is the great seeker-figure in our traditions: he contemplates the heavens, he sees the world on fire, he looks within himself. In doing these, he discovers the entire Torah. All of Torah can be found within the seeker's soul, as the Hasidic commentaries on Avraham make quite clear. Sometimes all the commandments, the Hasidic masters say, can be found within a single act.

Avraham journeying back and forth to the Negev; opening his tent-flaps to welcome, teach, and learn from all sorts of travelers; silently climbing Mount Moriah, went on a journey to *enlightenment.* In the symbolic language of *kabbalah,* Avraham is the dawn; it is he who established dawn as a moment of worship. He is the light of morning, the first ray of love, the right or compassionate side of both the divine and the human personality. To be enlightened is naturally and graciously to be compassionate. As we open our prayers, we lean toward the Avraham-side of ourselves, seeking to bind ourselves to his all-embracing vision of light and compassion. With Avraham, the light begins to shine. He is not told, "You will be blessed" as he sets out on the great journey, but rather "be a blessing"—cause your light to shine on others.

But Avraham is not the beginning of the light. One of the most ancient Jewish esoteric traditions is that of *Or ha-Ganuz,* 'the hidden light.' The light of the first day of Creation, it is taught, was so bright that by it you could see from one end of the world to the other (even around the curves!). Realizing we mortals were not ready to live with so much light, God hid it, allowing us to discover it bit-by-bit, as much as each of us could handle. Where is the light hidden? In Torah, of course, which therefore is called *Oraita* ('light-teaching') in Aramaic. But it is also hidden within our souls. The study of Torah has to be a meeting between those two great sources of light. We speak of this in our Torah-blessing when we say, "Thank you Lord for giving us Torah of Truth, and for implanting eternal life within us." When those two lights meet, to mix a metaphor, we can make great music.

The light within our souls was all there in a super-concentrated form in the soul of Adam/Eve, the single as yet undivided being we think of as our first ancestor. All souls were there within that single soul. (You and I were there too, as Reb Zusha reminded the Rebbe Reb Melekh.) In the necessary, yet tragic act of separation between those two halves of a single self, so that they could be turned around to face one another, thus beginning the generations of human love and the propagation of the race, the light was greatly diminished. It was hidden behind countless veils of lust, jealousy, domination, and other evils too awful to mention. Indeed some souls saw it coming and refused to join in the great divide—these are the "gay" souls that still insist that the "other" sex is to be found within the self, not in a partner of the other kind. It was not the sin of Hava or Adam that caused the lights to dim; it was the fact of their separation that caused them to sin.

Still, the light was there. Kayin, the son of Adam's exile, was unable to see it. He looked for that shining of light when he made his offering, but he could see nothing. And so he killed. But, by the next generation, the light began to shine; humanity could not have emerged without it. Enosh (the name means 'human') began to call upon God's name; he began to seek the light. The quest for enlightenment goes back to the very beginning. Therefore, by definition, it is found throughout the human race, in all the traditions of Enosh's descendants. We, offspring of Avraham, are one major branch of that generational light-tree *(menorah)* that extends throughout humanity, but we recognize our fellow branches as well. Sometimes, in fact, as in our age, we give light to one another, lighting up *ner mi-ner,* one candle from another.

What then is our Torah, that which Moshe received and had passed from one generation to the next? It is a language with which we can give words to the hidden Torah, the one that has been there since before Creation. That Torah, manifest in the hidden light, present within each soul, is both so intimate and so powerful that it cannot be spoken. Moshe's Torah offers it the gift of words, that which tongue-tied Moshe struggled so hard to attain. But our language includes more than words: melodies, rhythms, forms of practice, means of expression, by which the hidden Torah, the deep divine wisdom within our souls, can come forth and shape our lives to make us into the best and most fulfilled humans we can become. Our inner Torah is locked away behind a doorway; our ancestral traditions are a key, allowing us to open that inner part of ourselves and thus to shape a path of wise and gentle living. That is the life of service, *'avodah,* which is the way of Israel.

We are a covenanted community, 'standing under oath since Sinai,' sworn to serve as channels through which wisdom and blessing may pass into the world. Our devotion to that covenant is the real work that each of us has to do. It needs to be manifest throughout our lives: in our family relations, in our choices of profession, in our forms of rest, in the generosity (of both pocket and spirit) with which we give to others. Understanding that to be a Jew means to live in that covenant, to 'work on oneself' constantly to bring in more light and help it to shine forth, is what we have to teach. Some will do the work in a more contemplative form, some in passionate worship, still others is selfless devotion to others. All are needed, each one *ke-fum ovanta de-libba,* according to the call of his/her own heart. The community will draw them all together, have them nurture one another as we prepare to go forward and take the work to others.

We need, now more urgently than ever, to create communities devoted to that work.

A Letter on Meditation
The Practice of Hitbonenut
in Ḥabad Hasidism

Rabbi Miles Krassen

"A Letter on Meditation" is based on several such letters written by the sixth Lubavitcher Rebbe, Rabbi Yosef Yitzhak Schneersohn, published in the collection of his correspondence, Iggeret ha-Kodesh. Here, Rabbi Miles Krassen, one of the foremost exponents of Jewish meditation today, retains the epistolary form and gives us a modern presentation of hitbonenut, an important contemplative technique from the Ḥabad Hasidic tradition.

— N.M-Y., editor

Dear Seeker:

Thank you for raising the question of the lack of meaning you are finding in your attempts to practice Judaism. You say that you are finding more spiritual value and meaning in practicing the various types of meditation that are so accessible to us in our contemporary culture. You wonder whether 'meditation' has a place in Judaism, and what that place may be. This is a question that concerns many of us today. To answer this question requires deep reflection and an understanding of who we are, what we can become, and the methods available to us in our tradition for affecting the desired goals.

I. Judaism and Meditation

Let's begin with your feeling of meaninglessness in conventional Jewish teachings and practice. This is a very important issue that may concern us not only once, but periodically throughout the course of our lives, as we develop and grow into new levels of depth and understanding of the nature of life itself. There comes a moment in the lives of all sensitive souls when the conventional forms and practices of religion may no longer work for us. Whenever that occurs, here are a few things to consider. Our Jewish tradition has lovingly and faithfully preserved holy texts and teachings, some of which originated more than 2,000 years ago. It has always been a principle of Judaism to provide a vessel that can hold an entire community, composed of persons of all ages and types. For that reason, our Torah has often been said to conceal more than it reveals. Whenever we reach a point in life where the teachings and practices known to us become dry and uninspiring, it usually means that we need to look deeper. We have to find a way to enter into a dimension of Torah that addresses our newly emerging level of consciousness.

The evolving process of gradually revealing more of the hidden levels of Torah has been developing during the entire history of Judaism. In ancient Israel, it was associated with the Schools of the Prophets. Prophetic consciousness was able to transcend and see beyond the less evolved, conventional practice and understanding of the sacrificial cult. Thus, the prophets began the process of opening deeper levels of consciousness and revealing deeper dimensions of divine truth within the very depths of the human heart. With every new stage of revelation, a deeper dimension and level of meaning of Torah entered our world. As the Zohar, that inspired 13th century Spanish collection of teachings concerning the inner meaning of Torah and Judaism, puts it: "The Holy One, the Torah, and Israel are One." In every generation, as Israel, representing human understanding and development, evolves, a new level of meaning in Torah is revealed, and with it a deeper relationship to and understanding of the Ultimate One. Thus drawing out new, deeper, and more evolved meanings of Torah is one of the most important objectives of Jewish divine service.

This evolving process of uncovering deeper levels of hidden truth is not just history, it is the nature of every sincere seeker's individual spiritual experience. Spiritual life is dynamic. It has a pattern to it: seeking, finding, seeking, finding . . . The contemplative process of deeply looking into the meaning of our sacred texts and teachings in order to find for oneself their concealed truths is called *hitbonenut*. However, *hitbonenut* must not be mistaken for a merely intellectual exercise. Although, in the course of practicing *hitbonenut*, deeper understandings of sacred texts and concepts occur, the real purpose of this process is the power *hitbonenut* has to arouse the Heart. As such, *hitbonenut* is not only a practice that can reveal deeper meaning, but in doing so, touches that place in a person's Heart, in which one feels directly an inherent connection to the Divine Reality. The revelation of the Divine in the Heart has implications.

Hitbonenut is a type of meditation that not only reveals, but inspires.

In our generation, we are the spiritual heirs of the East European Hasidic tradition. At the very root of that teaching is the mystery of the Presence of the Divine in everything, everywhere, and always. The Ba'al Shem Tov and his students thus began to reveal in the 18th-century, a dimension of Torah that was more inclusive, monistic, and integrative than any prior revelation. It is precisely this teaching of Divine Presence that it is most incumbent on us to focus on in our *hitbonenut* today. We need to experience the revelation directly in our minds and hearts, and to reveal its implications even more deeply, clearly, and extensively in our own time.

II. How Do We Practice Hitbonenut?

If you are used to thinking of meditation only as a practice of emptying the mind, you may find it strange to think of *hitbonenut* as a type of meditation, but that is exactly what it is. Keep in mind something Reb Zalman has revealed (to paraphrase his translation of a line from our Aleynu prayer) "some worship You as Emptiness (shunyata) and we (the Jews) worship (the same) You as Loving and Abiding Presence." Judaism tends to emphasize and clarify the ways in which the Ultimate, "G-d," is present within the abundant divine display that we call the Kosmos. As such, a quintessential form of Jewish meditation, like *hitbonenut,* focuses on the particular ways in which the Divine is present in its various levels of manifestation. When we recognize and understand deeply the details of divine manifestation while in a state of meditative clarity and concentration, there is a very powerful effect that amazes and motivates.

Hitbonenut, then, means highly focused and sustained concentration on the implications of some deep concept, concerning the nature and function of the Divine as it is present within consciousness and the manifest Kosmos. Such concepts are particularly accessible to us in the revealed teachings of the Kabbalah, as interpreted by the Hasidic masters. Let's look more closely at the practice.

For *hitbonenut* to work as meditation, thought has to be 'highly focused.' That means the 'object of meditation,' a particular concept of the Divine, has to be selected in advance and the mind has to concentrate on that topic to the exclusion of all else. In order to enter into so concentrated a state, certain preliminaries can be helpful. It is absolutely necessary to clear the mind of any other interests and concerns. To achieve this, a still and comfortable body position is a prerequisite. Successful *hitbonenut* requires stabilization in a state of equipoise, the kind of balanced and integrated condition that Buddhists call *shamatha.* To help enter into this condition, focusing on the breath can be very helpful. In order to bring even more of ourselves consciously into the process, a short period of chanting a special contemplative melody *(niggun)* can be particularly effective. Contemplative chant gradually stills the mind and brings it into a relaxed, clear and open state that can be easily focused and held on the object of meditation. Moreover, the *niggun* draws the affects of the Heart into a more integrated relationship with the mind. Even before beginning the chant it is often helpful to intentionally turn one's attention towards the Divine Presence. Thus the preliminary stages are:

1. *Kavvanah:* intentionally opening to a state of awareness of being in the Presence of the Divine.

2. *Niggun:* chanting to the Divine Presence until one feels that the Divine Presence is chanting within you.

3. *Yishuv ha-Da'at:* using the energy that remains after chanting to produce a state of physical, emotional, and mental stability.

Once the preliminaries have had their intended effect, it is possible to begin to focus the mind on some appropriate and significant concept. However, focusing the mind is only the beginning of *hitbonenut.* The process itself involves sustained thinking to draw into consciousness all the levels of unrevealed meaning, concealed within the depths of the concept itself. For a beginner, sustaining thought on a single divine concept is no easy matter. The reason is that in order to sustain thought on a concept, you have to already have a lot of internalized knowledge, especially of Kabbalah and its Hasidic interpretation. The more deep Torah a person learns and internalizes, the better equipped one is for this practice. Thus, for a beginner, it is often best to choose specific and familiar prayers and verses from the psalms as the subject to be meditated on during *hitbonenut.*

A good way to begin the practice is to choose an important prayer text that one knows by heart. Then it is easier to sustain it in prolonged *hitbonenut.* The process involves deep reflection on each word and line of the prayer text. This method can be likened to squeezing juice from a fruit. One goes over and over every aspect of the sacred text, deriving and extracting all its nuances and meanings. As the meanings reveal themselves, there is a sense of stimulation, meaning, and even excitement as greater depths are revealed from within the text. However, this excitement cannot be mere intellectual (abstract) excitement of the mind. To practice *hitbonenut,* one must stay focused on the divine light that is present within every holy text and teaching. It is the increasing disclosure of that divine light that thrills the Heart as it is revealed within the mind. This occurs because one continues to draw out implications that are personally meaningful, accessible, and applicable to one's own experience. As the process continues, there is a growing sense of clarity. One feels that a hidden depth of meaning has been disclosed and can be held in its revealed form within one's own consciousness, without any further need for reflection or effort. At the same time, the revealed light is experienced as a heightened awareness of the Presence.

Successful *hitbonenut* has several important effects. It discloses meaning hidden within our sacred tradition in a personally accessible and usable form. It thus stimulates and inspires a person towards further efforts and growth in the spiritual process of development. *Hitbonenut* also discloses a feeling of Divine Light within the Heart, thus strengthening one's sense of the proximity of the Divine Presence. While one is practicing *hitbonenut,* this disclosure may even sometimes lead to experiences of *bittul,* in which one's sense of independent existence may dissolve completely into the Unlimited Divine Light. However, that is not really the purpose of the practice. *Hitbonenut* is more about the disclosure of the Presence of the Divine within manifestation and human experience. Thus, it is particularly effective for someone who seeks guidance concerning how to become a more effective agent of the Divine Will within the realm of embodied existence itself.

III. What are the Main Types and Uses of Hitbonenut?

There are two main types of *hitbonenut,* which differ in terms of the focus of the practice and the effects that result. We can think of them as 'big-picture' or 'forest' *hitbonenut,* and 'close up' or 'trees' *hitbonenut.* In the first case, the emphasis is on getting the gestalt of the subject, a general impression of the 'whole,' without looking too deeply into all of the details. It can be compared to a sketch that clearly conveys the general impression of the subject. With this method, one fairly quickly comes to the 'aha,' but the impression doesn't penetrate very deeply into the consciousness of the meditator. Thus its effects are short-lived. While one does get a sense of the 'big-picture,' the impression isn't deep enough and doesn't last long-enough to have a powerful transformative effect.

In the more detailed form of *hitbonenut*, the object of meditation is contemplated in a much more specific way. As such, it has the power to produce a deeper and longer-lasting impression.

However, the danger here is that in contemplating all the 'varieties of trees,' one may lose sight of the 'forest' and miss the most awesome 'aha.' The best policy, therefore, is to combine both methods in one dialectical process. One repeatedly moves back and forth in the mind from the big-picture gestalt to the detailed contemplation of implications, and then back to the big-picture, etc. This process is analogous to the dialectical relationship between *Hokhmah* (Wisdom) and *Binah* (Understanding). Through this process, the hidden depths of *Keter* (Divine Source/ Will) can be gradually drawn out and are revealed as *Da'at*, the state that manifests when the 'hidden' is grasped and held in the consciousness of the meditator. At that stage, one feels that one has 'gotten it.' Along with the lucidity in the mind, a palpable effect on the heart is felt and the *hitbonenut* process is complete.

In addition to the two types of *hitbonenut*, a distinction can also be made concerning the nature of the concepts that one chooses as objects of meditation. *Hitbonenut* can work as a meditation that is related to 'Divine secrets,' and as a method for working on refining one's character and personality. In the first case, objects of meditation would include any of the following examples:

1. *Memaley kol olmin:* the Divine light that fills all levels of manifestation.

2. *Sovev kol olmin:* the Divine Light that everything that

appears is within.

3. *Tzimtzum:* the explanation of how multiplicity arises from non-duality.

4. *Atzmut Ain-Sof* and *Or Ain-Sof:* the Ultimate in its essential nature compared to its unlimited radiance.

5. *ABY"A:* the four principal cosmological categories.

'Divine secrets' are primarily cosmological, psychological, or theological. In general, they address the mystery of sacred monism and the mystery of evolving stages of consciousness.

When the practice of *hitbonenut* deals with one of the 'Divine secrets,' it can produce a kind of spiritual nectar that illuminates the intellect. This type of *hitbonenut* is essential for revealing hidden truths concerning the true nature of existence. Most of the opinions and beliefs in our 'lower minds' tend to be based on what we can understand of the world that appears to us by way of sense impressions. Deeper truths are not generally accessible to the 'lower mind' by way of its habitual experience, but have to be received from a deeper/higher source. That revelation is facilitated by *hitbonenut,* which provides the 'lower mind' with insights into the concealed and deeper meaning of our sacred teachings. As these insights are revealed, the understanding of the 'lower mind' gradually deepens, until the very nature of what it experiences as 'world' is transformed. In place of a 'world' composed of seemingly independently existing 'objects,' one begins to recognize and appreciate the truly Divine nature of all that appears, without exception.

In addition to 'Divine secrets,' teachings related to refinement of character traits and behavior are also important as sources for objects of meditation in the practice of *hitbonenut.* In this case, one reflects deeply on a teaching that deals with a particular character trait. It is especially useful to contemplate the attribute, as expressed by the Divine itself, until a deep understanding of its implications arouses the heart. Inspiration for this type of *hitbonenut* can be found not only in the teachings of the Hasidic masters, but also in the classic works of mystical *mussar,* like the

Palm Tree of Devorah by Rabbi Moshe Cordovero.

Some important topics that can be used in this type of hitbonenut include:

1. *Ahavah:* the Divine nature of love and how it may be expressed in human experience.

2. *Yirah:* how to act with a sense of awe and ultimate respect for the Divine nature of all that exists.

3. *Anavah:* how to be aware of one's self as a particular ray, deriving from the One exclusive source of All.

4. *Tif eret:* how to bring beauty and balance to everything that one does.

In this type of *hitbonenut,* the goal is to feel the attribute as strongly as possible in the heart as the clearest understanding of its meaning appears in the mind. The result of such *hitbonenut* can be an arousal of a powerful motivation to cultivate an appropriate transformation of character, along with a clear idea of how that is to be accomplished.

IV. WHEN TO PRACTICE HITBONENUT?

There are three times when *hitbonenut* can be practiced with greatest effect. Since sustained *hitbonenut* internalizes the deeper meaning of whatever topic is chosen as the object of meditation, it can be very effective to practice *hitbonenut* immediately after studying Torah. Then both the form of the lesson and its inner meaning can be deeply absorbed. In this case, the practice consists in reviewing the entire subject internally, while maintaining a deeply concentrated state. As an aide to concentration, a contemplative *niggun* can be chanted or hummed without words.

Such a practice can greatly aid a student not only in uncovering deeper insights, but also helps to establish the teaching in the memory, so that it can be more easily recalled.

Perhaps even more important is to connect *hitbonenut* to prayer practice. Here one can exploit the power of *hitbonenut* to arouse a person into a more energized devotional state. Practicing *hitbonenut* before beginning a prayer service is a particularly useful way to prepare for prayer. Such a practice is especially recommended, before *davvenen* (prayer) with a *minyan.* In such cases of communal prayer, it is not always possible to introduce *hitbonenut* into the prayer service itself. But if *hitbonenut* is practiced for about half an hour, before the service begins, it can serve as a means of tuning the heart.

Ideally, when one has become proficient at *hitbonenut,* the practice can be brought into the flow of the prayer service itself. This is especially recommended when one davvens alone and there is no pressure to keep up with the pace of the communal worship service. Then one is free to contemplate the inner meaning of any of the prayers. This can produce a powerful inner arousal that inspires a person to draw closer and closer to the Presence.

Ultimately, it is my hope and prayer that all who read this letter will be moved to practice *hitbonenut* in whatever form is most appropriate. I hope that this practice will contribute significantly to the authenticity of your quest to draw closer to the True and the Real. May it provide a key to the innermost depths of every heart and consciousness, disclosing the channels of Divine Light and Love in our time and in this very world.

CONTEMPLATION IN PRAYER
Guidelines for Contemplative Practice

RABBI RUTH GAN KAGAN

These guidelines for the practice of hitbonenut *or contemplation are based upon the 'resumes' or aphoristic summaries written by the sixth Lubavitcher Rebbe, Rabbi Yosef Yitzhak Schneersohn, and appended to the chapters of* Kuntres ha-T'fillah *or Treatise on Prayer, a work by his father, Rabbi Shalom Dov Baer Schneersohn. Here they have been revised for contemporary use by Rabbi Ruth Gan Kagan, the spiritual leader of the Nava Tehila community in Jerusalem.*

— N.M-Y., editor

1. CONTEMPLATION IS A spiritual practice of great value, particularly the discipline of contemplating God's greatness and exaltedness. This practice of contemplation (*hitbonenut*) is also spoken of as "beholding the preciousness of the Sovereign One," an essential cleaving of one's mind to God.

2. Your learning and knowledge are only a preparation for the practice of contemplation in prayer. Spend time in this practice, allowing it to reach your innermost self; only then will it have a chance of influencing reality.

3. While practicing contemplation, be careful not to be caught-up in new insights arising from the words of the fixed prayers. This would be superficial and would stop the affect from reaching your innermost self. In this matter, there is a difference between

experienced and inexperienced practitioners, hence the latter should be extra vigilant.

4. You should know that true service (avodah) is one of intense mental effort and great absorption, naturally resulting in an arousal of the heart. This is what is called "the attraction of the heart."

5. 'Knowing' (da'at) is an independent aspect of the mind whose function is spiritual feeling. In this 'knowing,' it is possible to feel a concept, since the locus of this feeling is in the brain. Only then is this affect, this arousal in the heart, true.

6. There is an affect in the heart which comes from associative thinking. The resulting excitement of the heart from this form of thinking is not very deep and soon dissipates. Remember that the most important thing is that the essence of Divine light will be allowed to shine forth in your mind, and this requires great effort. The advice given is to regularly engage in deep and concentrated study.

7. Don't fall into the trap of busying yourselves with overly subtle thoughts and intellectualizations. This is often due to the lack of dedication to truly deep thinking on the words of the Sages. Beware of the danger of twisting the Sages' words, transforming them with crude conceptualizations.

8. Prayer draws life into concepts, and especially in that which touches the analysis of the part of our soul that is called the animal soul, in which there are three general classes: the goat (stubbornness), the ox (excitability), and the lamb (submissiveness). This analysis is through the faculty of 'knowing' which is able to discern and separate.

9. When prayer is accompanied by this faculty of 'knowing,' then the Divine Light will become fastened in your soul. On the other hand, without this specific work in prayer, even though studying ḥasidut (Hasidism, which is called "the word of the Living God"), it is still possible to remain totally separate from God.

10. The true and Divine service of prayer breathes life into the observance of the Torah and mitzvot.

11. There are five preparations to the work of prayer:

    a. Remove every worldly thought and stand still in one place;

    b. While putting on and wearing your *tallit* and *t'fillin*, concentrate on *ḥasidut*;

    c. Admit to the bitter insufficiency of the lower self;

    d. Evoke great compassion upon your soul;

    e. Imagine that you are standing before the blessed *Ain Sof* (God without limits).

12. There are some who busy themselves with *ḥasidut* who are not fit instruments for it on account of their lack of spiritual feeling; as such, they mistakenly perceive themselves as whole. Therefore, they need to go through a process of repentance to break the crudeness of their ego-centered nature.

13. Note that even among those who do this spiritual work there are some who have not carried out the analysis and purification of their emotional traits. This is because they don't pay sufficient attention to the residue of negativity in themselves. This can only be achieved through great effort and many prayers aimed at a single trait.

14. The inexperienced who have not yet studied much *ḥasidut* are more apt to err. Therefore, they must surrender to the more experienced, study deeply, and focus all their efforts in prayer, in accordance with the recommendation to remove every worldly thought and to stand still in one place.

15. Surrendering to the will of God is something that is equally available to all; and with its power, you can watch over yourself in everything that you do and uproot your negative traits while training yourself in the good ones.

16. If you are a person who doesn't have much free time during the day, you should make a regular time in the early morning for the practice of contemplation *(hitbonenut)*. It is especially advisable for you to commit to regular study before prayer. The

effect of this study and prayer will influence your conduct for the rest of the day and will infuse life into your observance of *mitzvot.*

17. Be sure to study the *Shulhan Arukh,* the code of Jewish law regularly in order to know the precise actions to take in your daily affairs.

18. Be cautious that your studies should always bring you to the service of God. This is done though the service *(avodah)* of prayer, which draws life into the practical observance of Torah and *mitzvot.*

WISDOM FROM THE ḤABAD LINEAGE
Aphorisms of Wisdom, Understanding, and Knowledge

RABBI LAURA DUHAN KAPLAN

These aphorisms were originally collected from the talks of the sixth Lubavitcher Rebbe, Rabbi Yosef Yitzhak Schneersohn, by his son-in-law and successor, Rabbi Menachem Mendel Schneerson, in the book known as Ha-Yom Yom, *'From Day to Day.' This small collection, retold by Rabbi Laura Duhan Kaplan, represent but a small sample of Ḥabad Hasidic teaching and lore.*

— N.M-Y., editor

WHEN THE MESSIAH arrives, the value of the simple, pure faith in God that we practice will be obvious. Study and understanding, even of the most profound matters, have their limitations. But loyalty, gratitude, and the sincere profession of faith are boundless. Simple faith in God's blessed Torah and *mitzvot* can be infinite. The Messiah will grant us understanding of the actual greatness of simple, heartfelt, sober service.

It is written, "Know the God of your father, and serve God with a perfect heart." (I Chr. 28:9). Knowledge gained through profound study has only one purpose: to bring one to serve. What Ḥasidim call *avodah*—service—bears fruit in action. One learns to discern good from evil, refine the virtues and develop a worshipful inner attitude.

* * *

Without air, a human being cannot live. Human life depends on the air we breathe, and the quality of life depends upon the quality of air. One who lives in an atmosphere filled with Torah and *mitzvot* lives a healthy life. One who lives in an atmosphere of cynicism, in denial of God's reality, lives a diseased life. Such a person is always in danger of being further contaminated.

The very first step in therapy is purification of the air. This work is the obligation of those who are well-read in the holy books. They can purify air by passing it through a filter made up of letters of Torah. They can recite passages of Torah anywhere—standing in a store, walking in the street, or traveling in the subway.

Everyone who knows how to read the holy books should commit to memory some *Humash, T'hillim* (Psalms), *Mishnah,* and *Tanya.* One who has memorized holy writings can think, meditate on and recite the holy letters of Torah in any place and at any time.

* * *

In 5648 (1888), Reb Shalom Dov Baer of Lubavitch was chosen to serve as chair of the *Hevra Kaddishah,* or 'holy fellowship,' those who have volunteered to fulfill the precious *mitzvah* of purifying, enshrouding, and burying the dead. According to local custom, Reb Shalom Dov Baer was honored as such on Simhat Torah. He was led to the synagogue in the company of huge throngs. He gave the talk, "The Holy One of Blessing Does Not Impose Tyranny on Humanity."

At the conclusion of the talk, Reb Shalom Dov Baer said, "The rationalized intellect causes people to err in the realm of the spirit. In the end, those who depend on this intellect find themselves in great bitterness. Even people of great intelligence must set aside their minds and not seek rationalizations. Now that the footsteps of the Messiah can be heard, the root of all service is to turn away from reasons and rationalizations and instead observe Torah and *mitzvot* with simplicity and pure faith in the God of Israel. It is in the nature of light to attract. When one sets out a lit torch, all those who seek the light are attracted by it."

* * *

A tzaddik's slightest word or gesture creates an impression, never to be forgotten, on anyone who sees or hears.

In the Jewish year 5569 or 5570 (1809 or 1810), Reb Aryeh Leib, the Shpole Rebbe, also known as the Shpole Zeide ('grandfather'), visited with Reb Shneur Zalman of Liadi, the Alter Rebbe. The Shpole Zeide was 'all heart,' more so than any of the other disciples of the Maggid of Mezritch. The Shpole Zeide told how he met the Ba'al Shem Tov when he was three years old. "He put his holy hand on my heart, and from that time on, it has felt warm."

* * *

Reb Hendle came to Reb Menachem Mendel, the Tzemaḥ Tzedek, for *yehidut*, a Ḥasid's private audience with the *rebbe*. When Reb Hendle came in, the Tzemaḥ Tzedek said to him, "Zohar raises up the soul. Midrash stimulates the heart. And the tearful recital of *T'hillim* (Psalms) washes out the 'vessel.' "

* * *

Reb Dov Baer of Lubavitch, the Mittler Rebbe, once answered a question from a person who saw him in *yehidut*, saying, "Speak to a friend about your service to God and study together. Then you will find in yourselves two divine souls who together can master each one's earthly soul."

* * *

Reb Shalom Dov Baer of Lubavitch announced at a *farbrengen* (a Hasidic gathering with the Rebbe), "Whether one is learned or simple, one is commanded in Torah to put on *t'fillin* everyday. In the same way, whether one is learned or simple, one is obligated to think for at least half an hour each day about the education of one's children. Parents must marshal all their resources and do all that is in their power—if not more—to make sure that their children walk in the way in which they are being educated."

* * *

Sighs are not medicine. In and of themselves, they cannot bring spiritual healing. A sigh is just a doorknob. It can open your eyes and your heart. Do not sit around alone wringing your hands. Instead, arrange your service and do it well. If you exert yourself, you will be able to strengthen Torah and spread it. You will be able to bring others to observe the commandments. Work in the way that suits your skills—writing, speaking, or giving monetary help.

* * *

Reb Shmuel of Lubavich asked his father, the Tzemaḥ Tzedek, "What did your grandfather, Reb Shneur Zalman of Liadi, hope to achieve with the ways of Hasidism? What was his intention?"

The Tzemaḥ Tzedek answered, "The way of Hasidism is a way of love. All Hasidism should be like one family, loving one another as the Torah wishes them to do. The way of Hasidism is a way of life. Hasidism should invigorate and illuminate everything, even that which is not good. One should become aware of one's own evil and of how one can correct it."

* * *

Reb Shalom Dov Baer of Lubavitch used to say, "The exodus from Egypt was our release from bondage. The Torah's word for Egypt, *Mitzrayim,* means 'narrow waters.' In Torah, the exodus from *Mitzrayim* takes place when the Israelites break out of Egypt and leave it for good.

"Hasidism is also an exodus from *Mitzrayim* and a release from bondage. But Hasidism offers a release from bondage to the world that also leads back into the world. Hasidism liberates us from the spiritual limitations placed on us by earthly life. We learn to live in the world without leaving it. We separate from an unthinking everyday relationship with the world, correcting that relationship through Hasidic service. Then we come to see the world as it truly is—a design of God's blessed will."

* * *

The Blessed One gives us matter so that we may transform it into spirit. We must work with what we have. When we lack material substance, even the smallest offering to God prompts plentiful gifts in return. Thus, Reb Shneur Zalman of Liadi, the Alter Rebbe, said, "Two Jewish souls who use material things *Jewishly,* they are truly spiritual."

* * *

We are 'day laborers' in the service of God. Day represents light. Our work is to light up the world with the light of Torah. Thus, our work has three levels. We must study the manifest Torah and show love for the observance of *mitzvot.* We must attune ourselves to the inner light of Torah through worshipful service of the heart. And we must raise sober and sincere disciples who will be devoted, heart and mind, to the inner purpose of Torah.

* * *

Mitzrayim means confinement and limitations. When the human spirit is in exile in *Mitzrayim,* it is as if the divine soul is oppressed by the animal soul. The animal soul looms large, blocking the divine soul from expressing itself. It squeezes the divine soul into ever narrower confinement, till the divine soul becomes afraid to speak. Exodus from *Mitzrayim* is the removal of the limitations that cause this confinement. Upon liberation, the intellect and mind can shine, illuminating the heart with good virtues and charity.

* * *

Whoever unceasingly recites the letters of Torah, *T'hillim*, and *Mishnah*, wherever he or she is, causes profound effects. This person attains the highest revelations, is spared the painful shocks that accompany bodily death, and strengthens the existence of the entire world.

* * *

When Reb Shneur Zalman of Liadi was nine years old, he studied mathematics and astronomy. When he was ten years old, he made a fifteen-year calendar. When he was twelve years old, he taught Maimonides' laws of the new moon's sanctification. Even the Princes of Torah who were present were unable to follow him.

* * *

It is the duty of every rabbi to announce in public: "The pain and suffering we are experiencing are the birth-pangs of the Messiah. The Lord our God demands that we return to Torah and *mitzvot* in order not to delay the imminent arrival of the righteous Messiah."

By the grace of God's Blessed Name, we stand right now on the threshold of redemption. We must reinforce our ability to observe and remember even the most minute particulars of our communal religion and our inner faith. We must observe and remember all the customs without omitting the smallest detail.

* * *

When the Rebbetzin Rivkah (wife of Reb Shmuel of Lubavitch) was eighteen years old, she took sick. This was in the Jewish year 5611 (1851). The doctor instructed her to eat first thing in the morning; but she refused to eat before praying. First thing in the morning, she said her prayers. Only after her prayers would she eat her breakfast.

When her father-in-law, Reb Menachem Mendel, the Tzemaḥ Tzedek, found out, he spoke to her about it. "It is written, 'Live in my *mitzvot*' (Prov. 4:4). You should bring vitality and vigor to the performance of *mitzvot*! To do this, you must have strength and joyous aliveness. You must take care of your health. Eat something early. Better to eat to pray than pray to eat." Then he blessed her with long life. She was eighty-one years old when she passed on.

Reb Shalom Dov Baer of Lubavitch once told this story to a Ḥasid who visited him for yehidut. "This story is about joy," he said.

* * *

Immediately upon arising, one says *Modeh Ani*—I am thankful in your presence, God. One says this even before purifying the hands by washing them. This order of practice holds a deep meaning. No impurity in the world can defile a Jew's expression of gratitude for being in the presence of God. No matter what a person is lacking, no matter what debasement surrounds a person, their *Modeh Ani* is always perfect.

* * *

Reason and passion are two different worlds of consciousness. Reason is calm and settled. Passion boils chaotically. A human being must work to unite these two inner worlds. Then, passion becomes focused yearning and striving. And reason becomes the advisor to a life of service and activity.

* * *

When Reb Shmuel of Lubavitch was seven years old, his father Reb Menachem Mendel, the Tzemaḥ Tzedek said to him, "Even our human skeleton is a gracious gift from God! We human beings walk upright, with our heads erect. Though our feet touch the ground, we can still see the sky. An animal's skeleton is altogether different. An animal does not see the sky, but only the earth."

* * *

When we look intently at another person and they return the gaze, the very essence of that person's soul has been stimulated. This also happens with a mental gaze. Thus it was the custom of our holy parents and teachers to visualize their devotees using this mirror gaze. By contemplating them with love and devotion, the Rebbe would stimulate the inner energies of the Ḥasidim.

THE RABBI TURNED COACHMAN
The Work of the Ba'al T'shuvah

RABBI RAMI SHAPIRO

This combined teaching and story is based on a famous letter written by the sixth Lubavitcher Rebbe, Rabbi Yosef Yitzhak Schneersohn, to a son-in-law in 1936 from Purkersdorf Convalescent Home. Because of its bearing on the second Lubavitcher Rebbe, Rabbi Dov Baer Shneuri's book, Poke'ah Ivrim, *it was later used as an introduction to future editions of that work. What follows is very representative of the type of teaching given by the sixth Lubavitcher Rebbe, of course, as seen through the unique lens of Rabbi Rami Shapiro, co-director of the One River Wisdom School.*

— N.M-Y., editor

LET ME TELL YOU SOMETHING about *t'shuvah,* or 'repentance' in the Habad tradition; and about the commitment one should have to supporting others in their *t'shuvah.* The Mittler Rebbe, Reb Dov Baer of Lubavitch wrote a little book called *Poqe'ah Ivrim,* the 'Eye-Opener.'[1] Over the years, many people have wondered why this book was written in Yiddish rather than Hebrew, seeing as the latter was the language of teaching and the former just the

---

1 The Mittler or 'Middle' Rebbe was the second Lubavitcher Rebbe, Rabbi Dov Baer Shneuri (1773-1827). The title, *Poqe'ah Ivrim,* comes from Psalm 146:17: "He gives sight to the blind." Notice that the psalmist doesn't say, "God cures blindness."

language of the people. The truth is, there is no way to say why he did it for certain; but there is a tradition coming from Reb Yosef Yitzhak of Lubavitch that the book was written for Reb Shlomo Leib, the *ba'al t'shuvah,* or 'master of the return.'[1]

The *Poqe'ah Ivrim* is entirely concerned with *t'shuvah,* and *t'shuvah* was a great focus of the Mittler Rebbe's teaching. He was a *rebbe* who was devoted to his Hasidim; there are dozens of stories illustrating his concern for their spiritual welfare. He treated them with the attentiveness and care a devoted parent gives to the education and guidance of an only child. His love was so intense that it even threatened his health.

From infancy, the Mittler Rebbe suffered from heart and lung problems, and his style of ecstatic teaching often exhausted him. At one *farbrengen,* the Mittler Rebbe spoke with such intensity that the elder Hasidim feared for his life.[2] So they asked him why he put himself at risk in this way, and he explained:

> When my father asked me to direct the newer Hasidim, he said to me, "The right way to direct a Jew is to see him or her as a reflection of the primeval thought of *Adam Kadmon.*"[3]
>
> What does this mean? *Adam Kadmon* is the state of pure transparency in which the light of God flows through you without distortion. This is the rung of being we call 'Child.' On this rung, the love between God and creation is unconditional; there is nothing that one needs to do other than to be. Yet the Child longs to descend into the world of action and the rung of Servant where it can carry out the will of God.
>
> Now, you might think that the rung of Child and the rung of Servant are separate, the former being higher than

---

1 The story of the *ba'al t'shuvah* takes up the bulk of this letter. *T'shuvah* means 'return' and refers to the acts of moral and spiritual turning that reconnect you to your true nature as an emanation of God.

2 A *farbrengen* is a gathering of Hasidim with their *rebbe.*

3 His father was the founder of Habad Hasidism, Rabbi Shneur Zalman of Liadi. This was in the year 5550/1790.

the latter. But this would be an error. Hence, my father challenged me to see the Child in the Servant, that is to see that the Light of God, so clearly present on the rung of Child, is no less present on the rung of Servant; that being and doing are not separate, but part of a single reality.

Why is this important? Because a spiritual guide must be able to carry-out the work of *birrur,* 'discernment,' seeing clearly the essential nature and destiny of the persons being guided, and knowing how best to direct them in the fulfillment of their respective futures. In this way, the guide can see the negative influences of the past and the promise of the future, aiding the person to overcome the former and to fulfill the latter.

My father's injunction to see each person in his or her divine transparency applies to ourselves as well. We are to see ourselves as Child, even as we labor in this world of service. We are never to forget our own true nature as one in the One, even as we labor in the world of seemingly separate beings and things.

When I think on this teaching of my father, and realize the gravity of the task placed upon me, I cannot hold back even to protect my own health. I must attain the level of transparency that I might see others with the same clarity as I see myself.

There are many such tales bearing witness to the Mittler Rebbe's utter devotion and concern for each individual Hasid. Given this fact, is it really so surprising that he should write a special discourse for a single individual?

The specific theme and content of the first 28 chapters of the *Poqe'ah Ivrim* is *t'shuvah,* 'repentance,' and the last twelve (29-40) deal more generally with faithful business practice, compassion, honor to parents, assistance to relatives, the avoidance of stinginess and tale-bearing, of false and evil friends, and the need to set aside time to study Torah and to effect contrition. Both the subject and the date of writing place it in the period of

Reb Shlomo Leib, the *ba'al t'shuvah* of our tale.

May the One Whose name is Blessed illumine the intellectual faculties of our souls so that we may understand and become wise in the teachings of our sainted ancestors and teachers. May we, recollected in matter and spirit, stir our hearts to serve the Blessed One.

THE RABBI TURNED COACHMAN

The task of reciting a tale is not as simple as it seems. The holy *rebbe,* Shalom Dov Baer of Lubavitch once said:

> The Alter Rebbe was of the opinion that our *niggunim* (melodies) should arise as if of their own accord.[1] They should, in a sense, sing themselves, rather than be consciously sung by us. This is also true of recitation of any sort. That which arises of its own accord is far more than a recitation, and that which does not is merely an echo of what another has previously been said.

There was a man of great learning in the town of Beyeshenkovitch named Rabbi Efraim Zalman who was in correspondence with the greatest teachers of his generation. When he heard about the profound learning of the teenage genius, Reb Shneur Zalman (later of Liadi), he traveled to Vitebsk to see this prodigy for himself. So impressed was he with the wisdom of the young man that he even began to doubt his own learning.

In despair, he sought out the aged luminary, Rabbi Avraham Zalman, who, though blind, was called 'The One Who Saw Much,' and told him of his situation. Reb Avraham Zalman consoled him by saying that "there are always those greater in wisdom; and if this were not so, there could be no real learning in the world." Rabbi Efraim Zalman understood and left to become a student of the young prodigy, Reb Shneur Zalman.

---

1 A *niggun* is a wordless melody said to transport the singer into union with God.

Now, the wizened old rabbi, Avraham Zalman, himself had a brilliant student, Rabbi Yosef, who was not only a great scholar, but deeply spiritual as well. At the age of eighteen, he married a woman from Beyeshenkovitch and lived with her for 25 years, devoting himself to the study of Torah. It was during that time that he first heard of the teachings of Reb Shneur Zalman of Liadi.

So moved was he by what he heard of the rebbe's teachings that he vowed, then and there, to travel to study with the Rebbe. Yet, three years passed, and still his vow remained unfulfilled. He then overheard from his teacher how even the great scholar Rabbi Efraim Zalman credited the teaching of Reb Shneur Zalman of Liadi with helping him to understand Torah. Hearing this, Rabbi Yosef finally decided it was time to see the Rebbe. That first visit lasted an entire year, and for the next twenty years he immersed himself in Torah study and the spiritual guidance of the Reb Shneur Zalman of Liadi, visiting the Rebbe every two or three years for additional direction.

In 5561 (c. 1801), Reb Yosef's wife died. For a year he remained at his father-in-law's estate; but, despite the wishes of his family that he remain longer, he then rented a room from Yohanan the Blacksmith.

His in-laws insisted that he take a stipend from them to support his studies; but most of the money he gave to the local free loan association, and the remainder he entrusted to three wealthy citizens who placed him on a budget. Eventually, however, the money ran out, and Reb Yosef supported himself through teaching.

Three years after the death of his wife, Reb Yosef went to the Rebbe for spiritual guidance. "Do you know the six orders of Mishnah by heart?" the Rebbe asked him.[1]

"Yes," Reb Yosef said, "I make it a habit to recite them monthly."

"And do you know that the word *mishnah* has the same letters as the word *neshamah*, 'soul?'" Reb Yosef was silent. He had never thought about this.

---

1 Mishnah is the early code of rabbinic teaching, divided into six sections.

The Rebbe continued. "The Mishnah you repeat, but the neshamah you do not repeat. The soul never repeats, but moves on. Do you understand?" Again, Reb Yosef was silent.

"It is time for you to move on. You cannot stay with the past. Marry a woman of childbearing age and you will have a son with her. God will grant you a long life. But remember this, it is better for your soul that you become a coachman than accept the commission as rabbi of a community."

Reb Yosef was startled by the Rebbe's guidance; but more by the idea of him becoming a coachman than of him remarrying. "All my life I have devoted myself to the study of Torah," he thought to himself, "Am I never to apply my learning as head of a community? Can it really be better for me to drive a wagon than lead a community?"

When Reb Yosef returned to Beyeshenkovitch he was asked to marry the widowed daughter of Reb Nataniel the Scribe. The woman was young and owned her own grocery store. Four years later, the couple had a son, whom they named Abba Zelig.

When Abba Zelig turned six years old, Reb Yosef was offered a rabbinic position in the city of Lyeplya. It was then that he remembered the words of his Rebbe—"better to become a coachman than a rabbi of a community."

For weeks Reb Yosef agonized over the direction of Reb Shneur Zalman. Was he really to become a coachman? He sought out the coachmen of his town and learned what he could from them. The job was physically demanding and mentally numbing. After 50 years of Torah study, is this really what God had in mind for him?

Then he remembered the Sages' advice that each man share his worries with his wife. So he brought his dilemma to his wife. When she heard that this was the direction of the Rebbe, she said, "In the morning I will go to market and sell my pearls and fine capes. These will provide us with the money to purchase a horse and a wagon." Her simple faith carried the day. Reb Yosef, awed by her simple acceptance of the Rebbe's guidance, would become a coachman.

Yet his doubts lingered. His prayers where filled with the pain of having to abandon Torah for the work of a coachman. His heart broke over the thought of no longer being able to spend long hours with his beloved Torah. And then he remembered an old friend, Rabbi Hayim Yehoshua, the Coachman of Velizh!

Rabbi Hayim Yehoshua was another of the Rebbe's Hasidim, learned and wise, and with sons and sons-in-law well versed in Torah. And he had been a coachman all his life!

The following Sunday, Reb Yosef left Beyeshenkovitch to seek out his friend, Reb Hayim Yehoshua. Arriving in Velizh, he found that Reb Hayim had traveled to the great market in Nevel. For two weeks Reb Yosef waited for Reb Hayim to return. When he did not return, Reb Yosef traveled to Nevel, arriving on a Friday afternoon.

Reb Yosef had many friends in Nevel, and his reputation as a scholar made his visit a joyous occasion. All Shabbat long he observed Rabbi Hayim closely. His words were wise, and he was addressed by all as "Rabbi Hayim Yehoshua of Velizh," and never as "Hayim Yehoshua *the Coachman.*" And yet, Reb Yosef's heart still sank as he imagined his future career.

After morning prayers on Sunday, Reb Yosef asked to meet privately with Reb Hayim. He told him of his decision to become a coachman. At first, Reb Hayim thought he had gone mad; but hearing that this was at the urging of the Rebbe, he agreed to help him find a good horse, a solid wagon, and to train him in the task himself. "In two or three days," Reb Hayim said, "you will know this work inside and out!"

Within a few weeks, Reb Yosef had settled into a routine. Traveling from Beyeshenkovitch to the surrounding towns, he made it a habit not to run from place to place, but to be "as standing water." He would spend his nights away from home at an inn where he would devote himself to study. And if he were to go to a large city, he would add a day to his journey that he might spend it studying with the Hasidim of that town.

Between Passover and Shavuot of 5576 (c. 1816), Reb Yosef made a trip to Senna. On the way, he spent the night at a Jewish inn.

And, as it happened, Count Batzeikoff and his personal secretary were also staying at this particular inn. When the Gentile villagers heard this, the local priest and wealthy merchants insisted that the count stay with them. It was "unseemly," they said, that he should "reside among Jews." Unable to resist custom, the count left the inn; but his secretary, who was himself a Jew, remained at the inn.

The innkeeper introduced Reb Yosef to the secretary whose name was Solomon Gametzky. Seeing that both men were to travel on to Senna in the morning, Reb Yosef offered to take the man in his wagon.

"What time are you leaving?" Gametzky asked.

"After morning prayers."

"That is not *a time*," the secretary said. "I don't care if you waste your time in prayer, but tell me at what hour you plan to leave, so that I can wash and eat . . ."

"And pray?" Reb Yosef interjected.

"I have no need of prayer," the secretary scoffed.

"How can it be that a Jew has no need for prayer?" Reb Yosef responded.

Gametzky ignored the question, demanded the innkeeper find him a different driver and insisted he leave before dawn, well before the time of morning prayers. He then stomped off to his room.

That night, around midnight, Reb Yosef arose to engage in the midnight prayers (*tikkun hatzot*). Reb Yosef's praying awoke Gametzky, the secretary, who crept out of his room to watch the rabbi in prayer.

He was overcome with grief and guilt. As he listened to the words of Reb Yosef's prayer, his mind flooded with memories of his own childhood when he was called "Shlomo Leib," of his first wife and child, whom he had abandoned along with this faith, and of his marriage to a Gentile woman with whom he had three children—two boys and a girl—though only one son had survived childhood. He was filled with a great bitterness of heart.

He had lost his faith in God and replaced it with faith in reason. He had replaced "Shlomo Leib" with "Solomon Gametzky." He had become one of the *Maskilim,* the 'Rationalists.' But this had brought him no peace. He simply abandoned his old life, his God and his family. He became the manager of an estate in Chernigoff. He befriended his young master, and when the latter married the daughter of the count, he entered the count's service as his personal secretary. It was in service to the count that he met his second wife.

Unexpectedly, the innkeeper banged on his door. He had, per Gametzky's request, hired a new coachman to take him to Senna. But Gametzky was in no hurry to leave now. He gave the innkeeper some money to pay the new driver for his bother and said he had decided to stay a few more hours and travel with Reb Yosef. Closing the door, Gametzky suddenly collapsed in a fit of despair.

As Reb Yosef's prayers filtered through the walls of his room, Gametzky was torn apart with grief. The words, "with great love you have loved us," brought him to tears. Was he still worthy of God's love? The words, "cause us never to be put to shame," drove him into bed. Could it be that his shame could be removed? As the words of the *Sh'ma'* slipped through the walls, he felt himself vow to return to his first wife, his first son, and his God. He rose, found the innkeeper, borrowed *tallit* and *t'fillin* and returned to his room to pray.

When Reb Yosef had finished his prayers, he went to see if the secretary was ready to travel. The man, however, was ill, stricken with a high fever, and unable to travel. He begged Reb Yosef to wait for him to recover and offered to pay him for his time. The fever grew worse, and Reb Yosef attended to the secretary as best he could.

That night, Reb Ya'akov Leib, another coachman, came to the inn on his way to Senna. Hearing of the sick guest and learning that he was the secretary to the count, Reb Ya'akov Leib snarled: "This secretary to the count is Shlomo Leib, who now calls himself, 'Solomon Gametzky,' 'Gametzky the Freethinker,' others call him. He is a sinner, a heretic. And yet, ever since becoming secretary to the count, he has been an advocate for justice regarding the Jews. So there maybe there is some good left in him."

Reb Yosef, hearing what Reb Ya'akov Leib had to say, returned to Solomon Gametzky's room. Reb Yosef said he had learned a bit about the man and wished to know more. The secretary asked Reb Yosef to call him "Shlomo Leib," and told him his life story and vowed to make *t'shuvah.* He remembered his wife and children. He wondered whether they still were alive and of what their life would now consist. How much shame they must have borne for his sake. How much they must have hungered, and all for what? He knew he must divorce his current wife and return home to his first; but it seemed impossible. "Must I harm her to rectify things!" He asked that Reb Yosef help him with the morning prayers, and then, at their conclusion, Shlomo Leib fell into a feverish delirium.

Reb Yosef could not in good conscience leave the man; so he made arrangements with Ya'akov Leib to carry his cargo on to Senna, while he, Reb Yosef, remained in the inn to nurse Shlomo Leib back to health.

At noon, a carriage carrying Rabbi Yitzhak Zelig Polotzker, known as "the Healer," stopped at the inn. At the innkeeper's request, the Healer attended to Shlomo Leib, but his medicines had no effect. The fever worsened, and Shlomo Leib neared death.

When word of his secretary's illness reached Count Batzeikoff, the count sent his personal physician to the inn. "Do whatever you can for Solomon," the Count ordered, "but do not trouble him with the news of the accidental drowning of his wife and son. It will be too much for him to bear."

When he arrived, the doctor quickly diagnosed the problem as an inflammation of the brain. There was nothing he could do. Reb Yosef undertook a 48-hour fast on Shlomo Leib's behalf until Shabbat. After Shabbat, he fasted again for 72 hours. Shlomo Leib began to recover.

In the meantime, the people in the inn had learned of the

boating accident that killed the secretary's new wife and son. Their bodies were never found. When Reb Yosef was told of this, he returned to Shlomo Leib's room alone. Closing the door behind him, he walked over the Shlomo's bedside, bent by his terrible duty.

Slowly and gently, he told Shlomo Leib of the death of his second wife and son. Three times Shlomo Leib asked him to repeat it. Finally, the realization hit him and he wept bitterly for them. When the tears stopped, he looked up and said, "Blessed be the true Judge." He could not escape the feelings of guilt that assailed him; but knew now that there was only one direction in which to go . . . forward. He would go forward and do what he could to 'return.' That evening, the doctor came to see his patient. What he found left him speechless. Shlomo Leib had recovered fully, requested that he be moved to a larger room, and then filled the room with a *minyan*.

The doctor sent word to the count that his secretary had rallied. The count then sent a wagon to take his secretary to Vitebsk to see the doctors there, to make sure he was well and fit. Shlomo Leib asked Reb Yosef to accompany him to Vitebsk, but he refused, returning instead to his wife and child waiting for him in Beyeshenkovitch.

Arriving home, Reb Yosef found a group of Hasidim preparing to travel to Lubavitch to honor the new rebbe, Mittler Rebbe, Reb Dov Baer of Lubavitch, who had taken over at the death of his father, Reb Shneur Zalman of Liadi. Reb Yosef rented his horse and wagon to another coachman and joined the group of forty leaving for Lubavitch. As they traveled, others joined them. By the time they reached Vitebsk, they numbered 180. There were more than 2,000 visitors in Lubavitch that Shavuot, all filled with joy, finding that God had given them another great rebbe teaching a true way of life.

But, equal to his joy, was Reb Yosef's shock at finding Shlomo Leib Gametzky there among the crowd coming to honor the Mittler Rebbe! He ran up to him and asked, "How have you come to be here?"

"Count Batzeikoff met me in Vitebsk intent on sending me to the Ukraine on business to spare me the pain of learning of my family's tragic end. I told him that I already knew of their deaths and that I was sorry to tell him that I needed to be removed from his service to return to my former life.

"At first, the count would not hear of such a thing; but after several days he agreed, providing that I travel to Lubavitch to meet with a certain holy man and do whatever he prescribes for me. I agreed. And do you know who that holy man was? Reb Dov Baer, the Mittler Rebbe! Apparently, the count holds the Rebbe in great esteem due to the patriotism of his father, Reb Shneur Zalman of Liadi! The Mittler directed me in complete t'shuvah, helping me to leave the count's service and to reunite with my first wife and son!"

Reb Yosef was amazed and blessed Reb Shlomo that this wish be fulfilled.

For two more months Reb Yosef remained in Lubavitch. Near the end of that stay, he went to the Mittler Rebbe for spiritual direction. To his amazement, the Rebbe told him to become the successor of the late Rabbi Natan the Elder, the leader of the Hasidic Prayer House on Market Street!

Reb Yosef objected, saying that the Mittler Rebbe's father, the Alter Rebbe, Reb Shneur Zalman of Liadi had told him that he was to be a coachman rather than a rabbi. The Mittler Rebbe responded: "My father told me of this matter. And he said to me that 'Yosef of Beyeshenkovitch has fulfilled his mission. In order to save the soul of one Jew, it was necessary for the rabbi to become a coachman. Now, in order to benefit many Jews, it is time for the coachman to become a rabbi.' "

When Reb Yosef returned home to Beyeshenkovitch, he sold his horse and wagon, ceased being a coachman, and took up the position as spiritual leader.

The Ba'al T'shuvah

Reb Shalom Dov Baer of Lubavitch said:

There are times set for *heshbon ha-nefesh,* 'examination of one's soul.'[1] Each night, before you recite the bedtime *Sh'ma',* you should make a 'soul accounting' for that day. Likewise, a weekly accounting should take place every Thursday as part of your weekday *heshbon.* The eve of the New Moon should include a review of the month, and the entire month of Ellul, the month of forgiveness leading up to Rosh ha-Shanah, should be devoted to a soul accounting for the entire year that has just passed.[2] Those who fail to do the Ellul *heshbon ha-nefesh* can still do it during the final days of the month, the days of *s'lihot,* though these days are really devoted to the work of *t'shuvah,* making amends.[3]

Just as there are different times for *soul-accounting,* so are there different times for *soul-repair.* There is the weekday *t'shuvah* that follows your nightly *heshbon ha-nefesh.* This is the most common, though in no way the least important. Then there are five distinct periods of *t'shuvah* corresponding to the five dimensions of the human being— thought, word, deed, emotions and will, corresponding to the month of Ellul, S'lihot, Rosh ha-Shanah, the Ten Days of Awe,[4] and Yom Kippur. A sixth period of *t'shuvah,* for the four days between Yom Kippur and Sukkot, corresponds to the four letters of God's Holy Name *(Y-H-V-H)* which forms the spiritual skeleton of each human being.[5]

---

1 Literally, 'soul-accounting.' This is a practice of reviewing one's actions and making the necessary amends and corrections needed to keep one on the path of goodness, justice, compassion, and humility.

2 Ellul is the final month of the liturgical year leading up to Rosh ha-Shanah, the new year.

3 S'lihot is the period of forgiveness prior to Rosh ha-Shanah. It is during this time that one is to speak to people saying, "If I have hurt you in any way, knowingly or unknowingly, advertantly or inadvertently, I ask for your forgiveness."

4 The period from Rosh ha-Shanah to Yom Kippur.

5 The *Tetragrammaton,* or 'Four-Letter-Name' of God, when written vertically has the shape of an upright human being: the *Yud* is the head and neck, the

Pondering this, it is clear that *t'shuvah* must first entail returning to the right path in the present, repairing mistakes made in the past, and seeing that error is avoided in the future. We begin with the present. Only when we are firmly on the right path here and now can we deal with matters past and future.

Second, *t'shuvah* must begin with the garments of the soul: thought, word and deed. These are way we act in the world; these are the instruments of will and emotion, the vessels that carry will and emotion into the world. Of the three garments, thought is the most important, yet it is with deed and speech that we begin our *t'shuvah.*

This is not so difficult. Either we speak kindly and do justly, or we refrain from speaking and acting altogether. There is no need to speak harshly or do injustice. While the proactive kindness in word and deed is preferred, if we are not yet ready for this, we can at least refrain from reactive harm. This is simply a matter of self-discipline.

The difficulty lies in the realm of thought. The problem is that we think compulsively and without end. Unlike speech and action, which have moments of pause and cessation, we think ceaselessly. We may not be able to put an end to thought, but we can change the content and theme of our thoughts. Whenever we find ourselves engaged in negative thinking, we can shift our attention to positive words of Torah, repeating these in place of the other words. While thought has not ceased, the negativity has been replaced.

It is important to work on thought, for it is the primary vehicle through which will and desire play out in the world. Thought carries the message of will and desire to the garments of speech and action. Furthermore, it can invest or divest energy in the message and thereby skew the way one speaks and acts.[1]

---

first *Heh* is the shoulders and arms, the *Vav* is the torso, and the second *Heh* is the pelvis and legs. We are to see the Y-H-V-H embodied in every human being and thus remember that we are meeting the image of God in every human encounter.

1 For example, your soul desires love and connection. The thought that carries this desire to trigger word and deed can do so in either of two ways: it can come

Whereas thought focuses solely on the self, speech engages others. Speech is revelatory and aimed at others who are in some sense our equals. We cannot really talk to animals at the level we speak with fellow humans, for example. Speech also has the capacity to address and awaken another's will and desire. When speech is informed by holy thought, this awakening is holy; when speech is informed by selfish thoughts, this awakening is often unholy.

Action deals more with a person's relationship to things. In this way, speech is higher than deeds, and thought higher than speech.

The careful examination of one's thought, word and deed is very difficult and demanding. Few have the capacity to do this all the time. This is why the month of Ellul is set aside for this work.

Reb Yosef Yitzhak of Lubavitch, while meditating on this, remembered a teaching his father, Reb Shalom Dov Baer of Lubavitch had once given him:

> There is a law saying that a woman shall knead dough only with water that has been left standing overnight. Why is this so?
>
> It is not water's nature to stand still. Water naturally expands; there is haste, albeit a natural one, to the way water spreads. This water, however, is to stand over night. It is to attain a level of stillness. This water corresponds to our own grasping nature. We naturally seek to grasp as much as we can; this is the expansion of water. But if we are to knead the dough, if we are to give rise to the bread of life, we must be still and not expand, and not grasp.
>
> This applies also to *matzah* and *ḥametz*. *Matzah,* the bread of liberation and *ḥametz,* the bread of slavery, differ in only one letter: *Heh* in *matzah* and *Ḥet* in *ḥametz*. The *Ḥet* is made up of three lines with an opening below, signifying that it

---

from a positive place of self-love that attracts the love of others by speaking words of love and doing loving deeds, or it can come from a place of self-loathing and speak and act deceitfully.

is closed to higher matters and concerned on with material things. The *Heh* looks a lot like the *Het,* yet has an opening in the upper right hand corner, signifying that is can look above and well as below. Liberation is the capacity to let the higher inform the lower. Slavery is to focus on the lower alone.

Matzah represents humility, and *hametz* represents selfishness. Both *matzah* and *hametz* need water in order to exist. The water of *hametz* is the expanding waters of the grasping self. The water of *matzah* is the standing water of the humble self.

The work of *t'shuvah* is a kneading of the soul. If we come from a place of grasping, there can be no cleansing or healing. We must come from a place of humility if *t'shuvah* is to happen at all.

Cultivating the humility needed for *t'shuvah* is our focus during the month Ellul. Toward the close of Ellul, during the days of *s'lihot* we are to focus directly on the heart: our desires and emotions. The number of days of *s'lihot* varies according to the dictates of the calendar; but they are never less than four, allowing us time to focus on the four essential emotions: mercy, justice, harmony, and power. The latter manifesting in one of two ways: victory or majesty.[1] With Rosh ha-Shanah, we shift from the heart to the mind, from emotions to will. Reb Shalom Dov Baer says that the essential goal of Rosh ha-Shanah is "to accept the yoke of Torah and *mitzvot,* to bend the will to the Divine Will." But, he adds, "this applies only to the coming year. For, Rosh ha-Shanah is also about doing *t'shuvah* for the past year. The time for this is at the sounding of the *shofar.*"

The Ba'al Shem Tov explained the power of the shofar this way: A king once sent his children into the forest to hunt. Being young and inexperienced, they soon became lost. They called to their father, but received no response. Panicking, they began to scream wordlessly. Hearing their cry, he answered them. The

---

1 These emotions correspond to the *s'firot: hesed, din, tiferet, netzah* and *hod.*

sound of the *shofar* is our scream for help. We have lost all hope in our own power to save ourselves and call to our Father in sheer terror. It is this acceptance of our own helplessness that frees us from the past. We continue to do *t'shuvah* of the will during the days between Rosh ha-Shanah and Yom Kippur. We return to do the *t'shuvah* of the heart on Yom Kippur itself!

A TABLE IN THE
PRESENCE OF MY ENEMIES
Spiritual Resistance in
Thought, Word and Action

RABBI NEAL ROSE

This following teaching is based on informal siḥot *or table talks delivered by the sixth Lubavitcher Rebbe, Rabbi Yosef Yitzhak Schneersohn, during the holidays of Sh'mini Atzeret and Simḥat Torah in 5693 (1932). Rabbi Neal Rose, one of Reb Zalman's first students, and his successor at the University of Manitoba, gives an analysis of these* siḥot *based on the originals and Reb Zalman's English translation.*

— N.M-Y., editor

AN INHERITANCE

OVER THE YEARS, I've had the *zeḥut*, the profound spiritual privilege, of knowing and studying with a number of the Ḥasidim of the late Rebbe, Reb Yosef Yitzhak, the sixth Rebbe of Lubavitch. Three of them have had a deep influence on me and my family. These include the late Rabbi Menachem Mendel Schneerson, the seventh Lubavitcher Rebbe, the late Rabbi Shlomo Carlebach, and *l'havdil l'ḥayyim*, Rabbi Zalman Schachter-Shalomi.

When I first met Reb Zalman in the winter of 1961, he suggested that I study the *siḥot*, or table talks of his *rebbe*. Among these were a set of talks given during the 5693 (1932) celebration of Sh'mini Atzeret and Simḥat Torah. Since then, I have studied and taught many of these same sihot to students of my own.

In this essay, I use Reb Zalman's translation of the of Sh'mini Atzeret and Simḥat Torah *sihot* from 1932 which he titled, "The Power of Thought, Word and Deed," as well as the original talks (which are untitled except for the name of the holy day and date).[1]

THE AUTHOR OF THE TABLE TALKS

The Communists in Russia carried out a long and brutal war against religion in general, and Judaism in particular. Despite these efforts, Reb Yosef Yitzhak directed an extensive underground network of schools and other institutions. He was frequently jailed for his efforts on behalf of Torah, and by the time of his seventh arrest, he was actually sentenced to death. Due to international pressure, he was released and exiled to Riga, Latvia, in 1927. The Rebbe was partially crippled and suffered a speech impairment, although neither of these challenges prevented him from continuing his spiritual resistance against the Communists and their crusade against Judaism. I have heard many stories about those days from Russian-born Ḥabad Ḥasidim who visited with us in Israel in the 1970s. They talked about how they secretly studied Torah and observed Shabbat and the other Holy Days, how their wives went to secret *mikva'ot,* and how their children had received a good Jewish education in spite of the difficulties. When we asked specifics—*Who taught you? How did you maintain yourselves?*—they refused to answer. But these Ḥasidim were fortunate. Many others suffered cruelly, and even died for their fidelity to Judaism. The Ḥasidim that I spoke to

---

1 *Likkutei Dibburim,* Volume I. For reasons unknown to me, Reb Zalman has left certain sections untranslated. The numbers that appear after my citations are based on the numbering system used in Reb Zalman's translations. Another English translation is available in Yosef Yitzhak Schneersohn, *Likkutei Dibburim: An Anthology of Talks* (New York: Kehot Publication Society, 1987), 1-25.

credited the Rebbe for their strength, and for their ability to overcome obstacles.

THE TABLE TALKS AND THEIR CONTEXT

The theme of these *sihot* is resistance, and they revolve around the Hasidic notion of causation. According to them, all human endeavors begin with thought, which is transformed into speech (language), and finally becomes action (concrete reality). Each of these stages is a *levush,* a 'garment' of the human soul. Without these 'garments,' the soul cannot express itself. Reb Yosef Yitzhak strongly reminds his audience that each of these stages has a reality and a power of its own. According to him, it is vital to remember that thought itself has immense strength. He uses stories, metaphors and anecdotes to drive this message home. For the Rebbe, all of these ideas are directly related to the plight of the Jews in Russia.

When teaching the Rebbe's table talks, I generally use a three-pronged approach:

1. Orality: the story-telling quality of the text, which allows the reader to sense what it was actually like to be there (at the Rebbe's table) creating a type of virtual reality;

2. Spiritual Resistance: reading the text as an expression of the Rebbe's personal resistance to oppression;

3. Imagery: as many Hasidic and kabbalistic texts are rich in imagery, it is my belief that this imagery has the power to enlighten and heal.

ORALITY

Despite his reduced circumstances in exile from Russia, the Rebbe made *Yom Tov* for himself and his followers in 1932. In Riga, Latvia, the Rebbe tried to recreate the Hasidic world of Lubavitch and a life-space large enough to celebrate the Holy Days. In this strange environment, Reb Yosef Yitzhak encouraged his disciples to spiritually resist the terror and anxiety engineered by the Communists. His talks were inspirational, and he hoped his Hasidim would be strengthened by them to keep Judaism alive throughout Russia. Thus, I believe these *sihot* should be viewed as a blueprint for spiritual resistance.

It is customary among Lubavitcher Hasidim to do *hakafot* on both nights of the festival, and during the day on Simhat Torah. At each of these celebrations, the Hasidim sat at the Rebbe's table—eating, drinking, singing, dancing and making merry. Interspersed with these activities were the sihot or table talks of the Rebbe. The rituals, prayers, meals and talks all interacted to produce a profound experience of the Holy.

The table talks were probably transcribed by Hasidim present at the event. When we look at the printed text, it is clear that it is a written record of a 'living event,' rather than simply lecture notes or a written essay. This is an 'oral document.' Its language is a combination of both Yiddish and Hebrew and has an intimate quality. Hence, the term *sihah,* 'conversation,' is used for it. The transcript also contains short dialogues between the Rebbe and those present. Most of what is written in Yiddish are direct quotes from the Rebbe or comments by his guests. Thus, the printed page is a record of the interaction between the Rebbe and his followers.

When I teach the *sihot,* in order to enliven the printed word, I ask participants to treat the material as the draft of a one-act play. We begin by singing a *niggun,* a wordless melody, to set the mood. Then we use the *sihah* to 'role-play' based on questions in the text, itself. As we read aloud together, the group adds additional melodies in places where the transcript suggests a song might have been sung. We are, in a way, work-shopping the early stages of a play. Members of the study-group take on roles and play characters that we imagine might have existed at the table—the Rebbe, a Hasid from one place or another, a Communist spy dressed as a Hasid, and so on. This, I believe, breathes life back into the *sihah* experience.

SPIRITUAL RESISTANCE

My second observation is that the table talks are an expression of the Rebbe's spiritual resistance against Communism and its war against *Yiddishkeit* (Judaism). As I mentioned earlier, Reb Yosef Yitzhak was imprisoned and exiled because of his activities on behalf of Judaism. These table talks were given during his exile in Latvia. Those who banished the Rebbe hoped that he would disappear into obscurity. Instead, the Rebbe increased his resistance, working even harder for the Jews of Russia. Eventually, he left Latvia for Warsaw, Poland, and in March of 1940, he moved to Brooklyn in New York City, where he continued his work until his death in 1950.

These table talks belong to the 20th century's spiritual resistance literature. At the same time the Rebbe was speaking out against Communism in the Fall of 1932, Mohandas K. Gandhi was conducting his own spiritual resistance in India, carrying out a hunger strike while under house arrest in Bombay. His table talks were also collected by his students for distribution throughout India. Were these two resisters aware of each other's crusades? One can only wonder.

IMAGERY

Third is my personal fascination with the Rebbe's masterful use of language, and with his powerful imagery. In my study-groups, we would often pause to meditate on these rich verbal pictures and then we share our experiences. It is through the imagination that we enter the realm of virtual reality . . . finding ourselves, once again, at the Rebbe's table.

SPIRITUAL RESISTANCE IN THE THREE WORLDS

Earlier, I spoke of Thought, Word and Action as components of Ḥabad's theory of causation. In Hasidic thinking, they are also realms of existence referred to as 'worlds' or 'universes.' In the introduction to the table talks, for example, the Rebbe speaks about the universe of Thought as being a distinct plane of existence.

As I read/listen to him, I am amazed at his ability to transport his audience to many alternative realities, or 'other worlds.' The comments in the talks indicate that Reb Yosef Yitzhak saw himself as carrying on his spiritual battles not only in this world, but in all three worlds of Thought, Word and Action as well. And he hoped, by example, to lead his followers to do the same.

RESISTANCE IN THE WORLD OF WORD

Logically, I should first discuss the role of Thought in the Rebbe's spiritual resistance. However, from a teaching perspective, I must begin with the realm of Speech. What is especially amazing to me is that the Rebbe was partially speech-impaired. Yet, despite this, he used language in a magnificent way and his words took people beyond their normal realm of experience!

In the Rebbe's account of one particular arrest, he describes how his interrogator pointed a gun at his head and demanded that he recant his commitment to *Yiddishkeit:* "Many a man has changed his mind because of this 'persuader,'" said the interrogator.

Reb Yosef Yitzhak replied, "Only a person, who has many gods (passions) to serve, and only one world to serve them in, can be persuaded by your 'persuader.' But I, who have only one God to serve and many Worlds to serve Him in, cannot be persuaded by your 'persuader,' I am not impressed."

Despite torture in prison, the Rebbe resisted. He indicated that he did so by moving into the parallel worlds that he had come to know through Hasidic teachings. These flights into alternate reality saved him from those who wanted to "burn him out." And he hoped that his ability to transcend Worlds would be something that he could teach to his Hasidim.[1]

---

1 Zalman Schachter-Shalomi, *Wrapped in a Holy Flame: Teachings and Tales of the Hasidic Masters* (San Francisco, CA: Jossey-Bass, 2003), 100.

As we read/listen to the Rebbe speaking at the table in 1932, we too are transported to other Worlds. We encounter the realm of the angels, of great saints, and of the rebbes of the past. At moments, he even brings us close to the immediate presence of God. He tells his Ḥasidim that, "in the *ma'amorim* (discourses) of my father, one would often find the expression, 'to feel the Divine content.'" The Rebbe tried to remind his followers that they too could have this experience, that Jews have a legitimate right to "demand this and reach this." That is to say, to demand that God provide them with an immediate experience of God's presence. Jews have the right to storm heaven! Such a people, the Rebbe suggests, have the energy to overcome not only the Communists, but all of life's obstacles.

The Rebbe was an amazing storyteller, whose language mastery allowed him to make entryways into many places simultaneously. In one of the *siḥot,* the Rebbe reminds his Hasidim in Riga that they were "dancing with the Torah in *hakafot* (circles of celebration) that join them with all the Jews of Russia"! The Rebbe praised their *m'sirat nefesh,* their self-sacrifice, saying, "Such Jews are the object of envy of the supernal angels, and the exalted souls . . . for all of them envy the Jews for their great *m'sirat nefesh* which shows itself as pure simplicity and clean faith."

At this point, the Rebbe, dressed in his *Yom Tov* finery, banged on the table and shouted:

SUCH *M'SIRAT NEFESH* IS SO HOLY AND PRECIOUS IN ALL THE WORLDS! WITH SUCH JEWS, ONE SHOULD ENTER INTO *HAKAFOT* TOGETHER, AND IT IS VERY CLEARLY DEMONSTRATED THAT THOUGHT IS OF HELP!

In the original transcript, this quotation in Yiddish is set in reverse quotation marks. In Reb Zalman's translation, these lines are written in capital letters, exactly as I have it here. In so doing, he is using an e-mail convention. Namely, that capital letters are used for shouting! Both the Yiddish and the English notation systems make us aware that this is a very powerful moment, brought about by the Rebbe's words of spiritual defiance.[1]

RESISTANCE IN THE WORLD OF THOUGHT

Many in political exile have been forced to reduce their mission to 'mere' thought. Their great hopes are said to exist 'only in their minds.' All their longings and dreams are gone, and only the memory of treasured ideas remains. Some are, at best, consigned to memoirs. But this was not the approach taken by Reb Yosef Yitzhak. For him, Thought was the beginning of his battle with the anti-Judaism of the Communists. "Thought, I tell you, has real power." In fact, he reminds his Hasidim, "It is the first and most intimate of the souls garments."[2]

In order to prove this, he tells the story of Reb Pinhas Koretzer's letter to the Maggid of Mezritch. In the letter, he thanks the Maggid for remembering him or thinking about him. He indicates that at a specific moment on Yom Kippur he felt the Maggid's thoughts connected to his: "Many thanks to your honored holiness, for you remembered me and raised me up in your holy thought on Yom Kippur. Be assured, my holy master, that I felt it here at the very moment. As a sign to you, this took place between Minhah and N'ilah." The Rebbe then cites Rabbi Shneur Zalman of Liadi who teaches, "that in thought, one can be with another in his place."[3]

Reb Yosef Yitzhak would agree with Viktor Frankel that thought allows us to become free. When all else fails, says Frankel, one can invoke whatever attitude one chooses. Frankel call these "attitudinal values," and he provides examples of those who became healthier because of a change in attitude. In the same way, the Rebbe refused to change his attitude toward the future salvation of the Russian Jews. The power of Thought helped him plan and implement his strategies for resistance on behalf of the Jews of Russia.

1 Yosef Yitzhak Schneersohn, "The Power of Thought Word and Deed," tr. Zalman Schachter, Section IV.
2 Ibid., Introduction.
3 Ibid., Section V.

Thought, however, is not perfect. In what way is thought a liability? The Rebbe explains that once thought patterns are established, they are very difficult to change: "The liability is that in order to forsake a habitual manner of thought, one needs a great deal of work."[1] This means that one can become a prisoner of one's habitual thinking, becoming immobilized by old patterns of thought. The Rebbe cautioned his followers not to become trapped in wrong ideas, especially about overcoming the policies of the Communists. He encouraged them to take their thoughts seriously enough to turn them into action.

RESISTANCE IN THE WORLD OF ACTION

As we know, thinking has its limitations. Intellectuals often spend too much time philosophizing about matters of faith, while 'simple Jews' are not bogged down by philosophical speculation. These individuals go forward and carry out the *mitzvot* with full hearts, unencumbered by philosophical doubt or questions.

Rebbe Yosef Yitzhak quotes his father, Reb Shalom Dov Baer, who in a *ma'amar* (discourse) speaks about the simple person's willingness to do a *mitzvah,* "when a simple person comes to something in Torah, he is prepared to do it without preparations, without preface." The simple person is a paragon of self-sacrifice, of *m'sirat nefesh.* Unlike the simple person, the intellectual "considers and considers and finally his intellect will not agree to *m'sirat nefesh.*"[2] As such, the simple person is able to successfully resist the Communistic attack on Jews in the 'real world.'

The Rebbe talks about simple Russian Jews who go to the hidden synagogues to celebrate Simḥat Torah. These Jews dance and sing, and as a result become the envy of the angels and saints.[3] It is the prayers of such simple people that are most pleasing to God, and God will answer their prayers. Again, the simple person becomes the real warrior in God's struggle against the dark powers of the Communists.

1 Ibid., Section XII.
2 Ibid., Section V.
3 Ibid., Section IV.

The Rebbe ends this discussion with a cautionary tale about his great-uncle Reb Hayyim Avrom, a man of intellect whose philosophical mind did not allow him to follow the directives of his Rebbe (who asked him to repent in order to save his life). Reb Yosef Yitzhak continued, "Within two years he went to America and, as soon as he arrived, his wife became a widow, and his children orphans. When my father heard of this he was very pained." The moral of the story is that even a learned person should behave like a simple person and act decisively in the world of action, the 'real world.'

IMAGES FOR RESISTANCE

The Hasidim of Rebbe Yosef Yitzhak often told me that they would review the *sihot* of the Rebbe and hear his voice. One Hasid remarked, "his voice went with me." For me, however, it is the Rebbe's powerful imagery that awakens my soul and helps me find courage. Doubtless these images also "went with" the Hasidim, aiding them in their spiritual resistance.

PRAYER CREATES ANGELS

The war against Judaism in Russia was for many years led by the Yevektsia, the Jewish section of the Communist party. These Jews were often ruthless in their attempts to obliterate the observance of Judaism and eliminate observant Jews. Synagogues were closed or carefully monitored, prayer was ridiculed and people tortured. In the face of the war on worshippers, the Rebbe tells his Hasidim, "Out of every letter and word of Torah, and out of each prayer, an angel is created. Realize then, that during the Days of Awe, seventeen million Jews are praying . . . all these acts create angels. And then heaven becomes like a convention city."[1]

The Rebbe continued saying that although the words of the liturgy are the same throughout the Jewish world, the melodies differ from place to place. The music of the Russian Jews, he tells

---

1 Ibid., Section V.

us, "creates a tremendous impression," and the angles created by their prayers "take first place." The brave Russian Jews are, in fact, the object of envy of the supernal angels. These images became the inspiration for a determined resistance of "pure simplicity and clear cut faith."[1]

When I teach this *siḥah*, I use it as an imagery exercise. We close our eyes, breathe out three times and we imagine the letters of the *Sh'ma'*, one-by-one, each turning into an angel. Or we imagine each word of *Kadosh, Kadosh, Kadosh*—holy, holy, holy. These become truly amazing experiences, and we can understand why the Rebbe's images still "stay with" the Ḥasidim today.[2]

The role of imagery in influencing and healing people has been summarized by Dr. Gerald Epstein in the following way, "inner images are the inner language, the true language of the mind and can help us shape and create our own everyday reality."[3]

THE JEWS AS A POMEGRANATE

The Rebbe realized that Judaism was disappearing from the lives of Russian Jews. He therefore urged his Ḥasidim to adopt an outreach strategy. He hoped to resist the 'Russi-fication' of Jews by targeting individuals, attempting to influence their lives in small but significant ways. "One must take a Jew and speak to him, tell him to put on the *t'fillin* and to wear the *tzitzit*."[4] Even if the person does not continue to do this or that *mitzvah*, says the Rebbe, one need not worry because a soul-contact has been established. The Rebbe speaks of each individual Jew as a pomegranate. While the pomegranate has a thick skin, its innards are beautiful. But it can only be reached by slowly and patiently removing its layers. So the Ḥasid is directed to work with individual Jews, one-by-one, removing the layers that keep their inner beauty from view. The promise of this strategy, says

---

1 Ibid., Section V.
2 I have heard much about the power of the Rebbe's words and images form old Russian Ḥabadnikim in Israel.
3 Gerald Epstein, *Healing Into Immortality* (ACMI Press, 2010), 156.
4 Ibid., Section VII.

the Rebbe, is that one day all of the pomegranate-like Jews will become a *Pardes,* a vast orchard of living and practicing Jews.

Those familiar with contemporary Ḥabad outreach activities will recognize that it was originally conceived of as a means of dealing with the assimilating Russian Jews.

Final Farewell: An Affirmation of Faith

The *sihah* closes with an affirmation of faith in God as the Heavenly Parent. The Ḥasidim are going back to the 'real world' and need to take a spiritual survival-kit with them. So they go to the Rebbe for a parting blessing.

The last section of the table talk is exactly that, a blessing and an affirmation of faith. If I ever have an opportunity to fully transform this *sihah* into a play, the closing moment might sound like the following dialogue between the Rebbe and his Ḥasid:

Ḥasid: Honored one, in our conversations we talked about prayer, about the service of the heart. All of what was said seems to apply to scholars who spend their time in the synagogue studying Torah. But what about we who are busy making a living; can we really pray with a full heart?

Reb Yosef Yitzhak: The elder Rebbe has taught us that a person must center one's life in the inner reality of the soul. That way, all of what we do is viewed from the vantage-point of the soul's sense of reality.

Ḥasid: Please explain.

Reb Yosef Yitzhak: Look at it this way. A Hasidic businessman must conduct himself like the son-in-law of a wealthy businessman, who provides his son-in-law with a life-long scholarship. So when the father-in-law occasionally asks the son-in-law for help, he would gladly do it, knowing that he would shortly return to his studies. He has no anxiety about his future because he knows he will be taken care of. So it must be with a Hasidic businessman; he does what is necessary, knowing that the rest is in the hands of a loving and caring God.

HASID: Honored one, please keep my family and me in your thoughts.

REB YOSEF YITZHAK: May the blessed Name give a good livelihood to you and to all of our Hasidim.

(In the background, an upbeat marching Habad *niggun* is heard.)

The Rebbe wished to instill *emuna,* 'faith' in his disciples. He had a deep and abiding sense that God could be relied upon in all circumstances. Hence, he wanted his Hasidim to go into the world with that same awareness so that they would be able to resist—with all their being—those forces that sought to obliterate Judaism. In order for this to happen, they had to be trained to resist in Thought, Word and Action.

One God, Many Worlds
Living in the 'Four Worlds' of Hasidism and Sufism

Pir Netanel Mu'in ad-Din Miles-Yépez

Originally a talk given to a gathering of Inayati Sufis in the Spring of 2013, this teaching is based in part on a letter concerning the Four Worlds by the sixth Lubavitcher Rebbe, Rabbi Yosef Yitzhak Schneersohn. It was the first subject Reb Zalman ever asked the author, a student of both Hasidism and Sufism, to teach publically. It is published here in honor of him and in fulfillment of that request.

— N.M-Y., editor

In the Summer of 1920, *the Lubavitcher Rebbe, Rabbi Yosef Yitzhak Schneersohn, was summoned before a Communist tribunal to account for his so-called "Godly activities." During his interrogation, one of the committee members—annoyed by his lack of cooperation—said to him, "You had better think about cooperating." The Rebbe told the committee he would not depart from his principles. The man then lifted a revolver and pointed it at him, saying, "Many a man has changed his mind while looking down the barrel of this 'persuader.' " The Rebbe stared back at him and replied, coolly, "Only a person who has many gods to serve, and only one world to serve them in, is frightened by your 'persuader.' But I, who have only one God to serve, and many Worlds in which to serve, I'm not frightened." He was later released unharmed.*[1]

---

1 A favorite story of Ḥabad-Lubavitcher Ḥasidim that I first heard from Rabbi Zalman Schachter-Shalomi, z"l. A written account of the same incident is found in the diaries of the sixth Lubavitcher Rebbe.

Can you imagine having such confidence? The lives that most of us lead are so small. We live in just one tiny world and have so many 'gods' to serve—love, money, sex, attention—at whose altars we worship every day, often from moment to moment. We chase after every desire and run from every fear. How different it would be to worship just one God in all things, to worship "the Only Being" everywhere we go and in everything we meet, to live in realities that free us from the tyranny of such "persuasion."

But what did the Rebbe mean by "many Worlds"? On one level, at least, he was referring to something we talk about everyday. We say, so and so 'belongs to the art world,' 'the world of science,' or 'politics.' And when we say this, we all understand what we mean—overlapping worlds of special significance to those who take part in them—worlds with their own rules and symbols, like those inhabited by artists, scientists, or politicians. In this case, however, the rules and symbols belong to the metaphysical realities described in Hasidism and Kabbalah, the Jewish mystical tradition, whose terrain is mapped by spiritual masters like the sixth Lubavitcher Rebbe.

Nevertheless, the Jewish mystical tradition is not the only tradition to speak of other Worlds. In the mystical teachings of Sufism—sometimes called the 'tasted wisdom' *(hikmat al-dhawqiyya)*—we are also taught that there are an infinite number of Worlds in existence, of which four are most useful for us to understand, just as in Hasidic teaching. Though there are occasional variations and differences in their descriptions and number, there are also striking parallels between them.[1] Below, I will attempt to give over a synthetic view of these Worlds as they are described in Hasidism and Sufism.

---

1 "Our sages revealed from Scripture that there are universes beyond number. This means that each of them is an infinity in itself. The finite is not boundless, and thus may be counted. But since as we have it from Scripture that they cannot be counted, those universes are known to be boundless and infinite." Yosef Yitzhak Schneersohn, tr. Zalman Schachter-Shalomi, "A Letter on the Four Worlds."

KNOWLEDGE AND WORLDS

As both Hebrew and Arabic are Semitic languages, their words for 'worlds'—*olamot* and *'ālamīna*—are based in the same Semitic root, *Ayin-Lammed-Mem* or *'Ayn-Lām-Mīm*. In Hebrew, the words derived from this root generally have to do with things hidden, as well as great, undefined distances beyond the horizon.[1] Thus, the Hebrew word, *olam*, can mean both 'eternity' and 'world,' depending on the context. In Arabic, the words derived from this root also have to do with knowledge. So there is a relationship between knowledge (*'ilm*) and the world (*al-'alamun*) in Arabic due to the boundless nature of each in Semitic thinking. For, unlike us, with our modern tendency to think of worlds and knowledge as things contained, or containing definite constituent parts, our Semitic forbears looked out on the far horizon and thought only of how vast and undefined it was. Thus, their ideas of knowledge and worlds had these same characteristics—both were open-ended and participated in 'eternity.'

This is something that we need to keep in mind when thinking about the mystical Worlds of Hasidism and Sufism. For when we attempt to talk about them in a static way (as I am doing here), what we are really talking about is "their middle," as my *rebbe* and *murshid* once reminded me. We don't actually know where they begin or end; nor is it as easy to talk about where they meet and overlap. Thus, we are often forced to describe an idealized 'middle zone,' where the admixture of Worlds seems least evident, and where they are most 'themselves,' as it were.[2]

---

1 In an annotation to his translation of the sixth Lubavitcher Rebbe's "A Letter on The Four Worlds," Reb Zalman writes: "The Hebrew word for 'world' or 'universe' is *olam*. Hasidism teaches us that *olam* and *he-elem*, meaning 'obscuring' or 'hiding,' are related. Each universe, having its own dimensions, thus hides that which transcends it."

2 In his "Letter on the Four Worlds," the sixth Lubavitcher Rebbe writes, "And now it will make sense when we call the highest of the Four Worlds, *Atzilut*, a 'world.' By this we mean that it is limited within its own confines; because what we mean by 'world,' is that no matter how vast (or even infinite) the universe is, it is confined and bound to itself." Thus, it is not about its 'boundaries,' but it's essence.

This, of course, is an abstracted and artificial way of talking about them; but at least it gives us a place to begin. And really, that is all we are doing here—making a beginning. Thus, it is important to understand that everything that I'm going to say is merely heuristic, meaning that these are ways of talking about metaphysical realities that help us to understand them, but which are not to be thought of as definitive. My own understandings and descriptions will certainly differ from those of others who may see the "middle" differently, or who may have more insight and ability to describe the 'far reaches' of the Worlds. But the more perspectives one gets on the Worlds, the better; each perspective adds dimension to one's understanding and breaks the idols of certainty that we put in place of genuine experience.

THE FOUR WORLDS

For simplicity's sake, I'll use my teacher, Rabbi Zalman Schachter-Shalomi's terminology to help us grasp the more immediate parallels between the Worlds in both traditions. In his teaching, he would often talk about the Four Worlds as the World of Action, the World of Feeling, the World of Knowing, and the World of Being. In these, he saw the celestial archetypes responsible for the mysterious phenomenon of 'four-foldness,' or "four-sies" as he called them, found throughout creation. Thus, he liked to draw attention to the parallels between the Four Elements (Earth, Water, Fire, Air); the Four Functions of Jungian Psychology (Sensation, Feeling, Thinking, Intuition); the Four Yogas of Vedanta (*Karma Yoga, Bhakti Yoga, Jñana Yoga, Raja Yoga);* and the Four Levels of Spiritual Understanding in Sufism (*Sharī'ah, Tarīqah, Ma'rifah, Haqīqah).*

Let's consider the latter four for the moment. In Sufism, each of these four levels of understanding provides a foundation for the next. *Sharī'ah* is the 'well-trodden path.' It refers to the normative religious path of Islam and all that is required of a Muslim. This is the ground level, everything that a Muslim must do in the World of Action. *Tarīqah,* on the other hand, is "the trackless path in the desert that the Bedouin follow from oasis to oasis."[1] This is the Sufi path, requiring a spiritual guide who is intimately familiar with the landscape of the heart in the World of Feeling, and who knows the way to your ultimate destination. Following such a guide's direction, one's experiences things for oneself and begins to get a sense in the World of Knowledge of that landscape. This is what is called *Ma'rifah*, 'experiential knowledge' or *gnosis*. Beyond this is *Haqīqah*, the 'truth as-it-is' in the World of Being, which cannot be expressed in the ordinary world of duality.[2]

Nevertheless, Sufism also speaks of metaphysical Worlds that more directly parallel the Worlds of Hasidism and Kabbalah, and it is these that I would like to talk about in detail here.[3] In particular, I would like to look at them from the different perspectives of Rabbi Zalman Schachter-Shalomi (1924-2014), who often described the Worlds from a psychological perspective, and the Sufi master, Pir Vilayat Inayat-Khan (1916-2004), who looked at them as stages in the development of consciousness in which one is incrementally freed from bondage to the ego.

The World of Action

Of course, the World with which we are most familiar, and to which we most closely relate on a daily basis, is the World of Action or Doing. In Hasidism, this is *Olam ha-Assiyah*, the 'World

---

1 Robert Frager, *Heart, Self, and Soul: The Sufi Psychology of Growth, Balance, and Harmony* (Wheaton, IL: Quest Books, 1999), x-xi.

2 Most Sufi texts place *Haqīqah* before *Ma'rifah*, but this is really about how these are being taught. Reb Zalman preferred this schema ending with *Haqīqah*, where one's individual ego is wholly obscured by the Truth. Other Sufis emphasize *Ma'rifah* or gnosis as the result of having tasted the Truth. See Gregory Blann, *The Garden of Mystic Love: Volume I: The Origin and Formation of the Great Sufi Orders* (Boulder, CO: Albion-Andalus Books, 2014), 232-33. In Hasan Lufti Shushud, *Masters of Wisdom in Central Asia: Teachings from the Sufi Path of Liberation* (Rochester, VT: Inner Traditions, 2014), 173, *Ma'rifah* is presented as the unitive experience, and *Haqīqah* as Reality.

3 In as much as *kabbalah* was absorbed into Hasidism, especially as taught by Rabbi Dov Baer, the Maggid of Mezritch, and his disciple, Rabbi Shneur Zalman of Liadi, founder of the Ḥabad lineage.

of Making,' or the World in which we make and do things.[1] In Sufism, the same World is called, *'Ālam an-Nāsūt,* the 'World of Humanity,' the visible world we inhabit, the material world of the senses. This is the World we all know—though we might make one distinction. Jewish sources sometimes distinguish between what could be called the *'life'* of the visible world and its *'matter,'* often describing *Assiyah* as its 'life,' its animate or living quality.[2]

Thus, in his own teaching, Reb Zalman placed "the body and its energies" in the World of Action, saying:

> *Assiyah,* or 'doing,' is the designation for the physical world of action, which includes action for spiritual purposes. It is the world of the *guf* and *nefesh,* the body and its energies, located in the realm of sensation and behavior. The Jewish code of religious practice, the *halakhah,* operates largely in *Assiyah.* On this level, religion trains people in behaviors intended to please God by obedience to the divine law, and piety is expressed mostly through *g'millut ḥassadim,* doing 'deeds of loving-kindness' and observing the *mitzvot.*[3]

But *Assiyah* is also said to be the World that both conceals the light of Divinity *from us,* and at the same time, reveals it *to us.* This is because it is the most dense 'contraction' *(tzimtzum)* of the divine light, allowing for the illusion of finitude and separation, and thus also our general ignorance of the divine Reality. But it is also "a vessel that was made to receive God's light," being the "place where the spiritual actually interacts with the physical

---

1 As *Assiyah* is derived from the root, *Ayin-Shin-Heh,* meaning, 'to make.'

2 In *Adornment of Hearts* (Westport, CT: Pir Press, 1991), 49, Sheikh Muzaffer Ozak speaks of "The Visible World, the World of Gross Body." But the sixth Lubavitcher Rebbe writes in his "Letter on the Four Worlds," "Thus, we can also see that the lowest of all worlds, the world of *Assiyah,* which is also a spiritual one, and which contains no physical matter, deserves the same term, 'world.'"

3 Zalman M. Schachter-Shalomi, *Gate to the Heart: A Manual of Contemplative Jewish Practice* (Boulder, CO: Albion-Andalus Books, 2013), 14. Also "Kabbalah and Transpersonal Psychiatry," *Textbook of Transpersonal Psychiatry and Psychology* (New York: Basic Books, 1996), 123.

dimension."[1] That is to say, *Assiyah* is both materiality and the energies of the material universe blinding us to more subtle dimensions, and yet, is also our interface with those subtle dimensions.

Similarly, Sufism treats *Nāsūt* as the "fruit" of the divine tree, the place where we can interact with and enjoy the Divine Presence: "Some call it the visible world *(shahadat)* or simply the created world *(mulk);* others call it the world of waking consciousness *(bidar)* or the world-as-believed *(pindar)*."[2] In the school of Ibn al-Arabi, *Nāsūt* (humanity) is also understood to be vessel which contains *Lāhūt* (Divinity).[3]

Following on his father Hazrat Inayat Khan's description, Pir Vilayat Inayat-Khan likens our experience of the World of Action to a stage in the development of consciousness where one is addicted to sensory experience and caught in an egoic solipsism:

> *Nāsūt,* according to the Sufis, is the ordinary state in which we, along with most people, find ourselves. We think of ourselves as the subject who is observing the world as the object. We are in a state of dependence. [. . .] we identify with our body, our thoughts, our emotions, or our self-image [. . .] to evolve we need to be weaned from that attachment.[4]

---

1 Aryeh Kaplan, *Innerspace: Introduction to Kabbalah, Meditation and Prophecy* (Jerusalem: Moznaim, 1991), 27.

2 Scott Kugle (ed.), *Sufi Meditation and Contemplation: Timeless Wisdom from Mughal India* (New Lebanon, NY: Suluk Press, 2012), 137.

3 Saiyid Athar Abbas Rizvi, *A History of Sufism in India: Volume I: Early Sufism and its History in India to AD 1600* (New Delhi: Munshiram Manoharlal Publishers, 1997), 369.

4 Vilayat Inayat-Khan, *Awakening Through the Planes: The Developmental Stages* (Seattle, WA: Sufi Order International, 1998), 6, 7, 8. In Zia Inayat-Khan (ed.), *Caravan of Souls: An Introduction to the Sufi Path of Hazrat Inayat Khan* (New Lebanon, NY: Suluk Press, 2013), 124, Hazrat Inayat Khan says: "This is the consciousness dependent on our senses. Whatever we see by means of the eye, or hear by means of the ear, whatever we smell and taste, all these experiences, which we gain by the help of the material body, prove to us that this is a particular plane of consciousness, or a particular kind of experience of consciousness."

This is the trick of the senses, allowing us to identify with the body as separate from the rest of Reality. Thus, for Pir Vilayat, *Nāsūt* represents the generally limited state of consciousness which the World of Action engenders. And yet, this very tendency also creates the dissatisfaction with limited consciousness that drives one to seek a World beyond.

THE WORLD OF FEELING

Beyond the 'energy of life' in the World of Action is the World of Feeling. In Hasidism, this is *Olam ha-Yetzirah*, the 'World of Formation.' The sense here is of a sculptor forming and shaping soft clay with their hands. It hasn't yet reached the stage of drying and being baked in a kiln. It is still a plastic, malleable world. In Sufism, it is called, *'Ālam al-Malakūt*, the 'World of Angels,' the invisible world, perceivable only through the spiritual-senses.[1] This is the world made up of emotion, qualities, intentions, forms and spiritual energies, often related to the faculty of speech—all the aspects of experience that 'feel' tangible to us, but which are not quite that in the World of Action.

Reb Zalman writes of *Yetzirah* mostly from the point-of-view of emotion:

> The inner experience of feeling or deep emotion is in the world of *Yetzirah*, where we find *ru'aḥ*, the 'breath-spirit.' *Yetzirah*, which means 'formation,' also involves images, values and myths. On this level, piety is measured in terms of devoutness: the sincere feeling one invests in prayer and worship. Purification of emotions is one of the central tasks to be accomplished on this level, and is a prerequisite for full entry into the world of the Kabbalah.[2]

Likewise, *Malakūt* in Sufism is often discussed as the essential

---

1 Ozak, *Adornment of Hearts,* 49, "The World of Ideas, the World of Angels of Subtle Body."
2 Schachter-Shalomi, *Gate to the Heart,* 14.

entry-point into deeper spiritual realities. A number of terms in Sufism are merely synonyms for *Malakūt*, it being called "the world of spirits *(arwah)*" or "the unseen *(ghayb),*" "the subtle world *(latif)* or the world of dreaming *(khwab)*."[1] Moreover, some of these—according to one source, at least—are described differently merely to facilitate access to this World. For instance, the often-discussed World of the Imagination *('Ālam al-Mithāl)* is really, according to Dara Shikoh, the means to opening *Malakūt*, and that to "make this opening clear, it is described as different from the spiritual world and is called the imaginative world; but in reality the imaginative world is part and parcel of the spiritual world *[Malakūt]*."[2]

Interestingly, in both traditions, the World of Feeling is associated with angels: "The living creatures of the world of formation, the beings who function in it as we function in the world of action, are called, in a general way, 'angels.'"[3] Pir Vilayat suggests that it is necessary for one to enter into the angelic consciousness in order to experience *Malakūt*.[4] But this is perhaps better discussed in relation to the soul's experience of this World later.

THE WORLD OF KNOWING

Above this World of Feeling is the World of Knowing or Thought. Among Ḥasidim, it is called *Olam ha-B'riyah,* the 'World of Creation.' Among Sufis, *'Ālam al-Jabarūt,* the 'World of Power.' This is the heavenly World of divine names and characteristics, the World of Souls[5] where divine decrees are made and everything is planned before it descends into form and matter (Feeling and Action). Here is where the 'architectural plans' are made for

---

1 Kugle, *Sufi Meditation and Contemplation,* 139.
2 "The Compass of Truth" in Kugle, *Sufi Meditation and Contemplation,* 138.
3 Adin Steinsaltz, *The Thirteen Petalled Rose: A Discourse on the Essence of Jewish Existence and Belief* (New York: Basic Books, 1980), 8.
4 Inayat-Khan, *Awakening Through the Planes,* 41.
5 Ozak, *Adornment of Hearts,* 49.

creation, or maybe the sketch for the aforementioned sculpture to be worked on in the World of Feeling.

Of the World of Knowing, Reb Zalman writes in terms of 'understanding':

> The third level of reality is the world of *B'riyah,* or 'creation,' the world of thinking and philosophy, thought or contemplation, where we seek to understand the blueprint of the universe. This is where the *neshamah* [*soul*] is rooted. *B'riyah* also includes the faculties of concept, idea, hypothesis and theory. On this level, piety expresses itself in how one invests time and awareness in the study of Torah and the esoteric teachings.[1]

Just as *Yetzirah* below it is described as a World of Feeling or emotion, filled with beings of pure emotion (angels), *B'riyah* above it is described as a World of Knowing, or "pure mind." It is said, "This mind quality of the world of creation is not a merely intellectual essence but rather expresses itself as the power and capacity to grasp things with a genuine, inner understanding; it is, in other words, the mind as creator as well as that which registers and absorbs knowledge."[2]

Among Sufis, there is some debate about how this World is to be described. Dara Shikoh writes that '*Ālam al-Jabarūt* is called "the causal realm *('alam-i lazim),* but says that many Sufis err in calling it "the realm of names and attributes" *(asma o sifat),*[3] a description which would generally coincide with the World of Knowing as the locus of divine archetypes. Nevertheless, this is how we are dealing with it here.

Pir Vilayat steers a middle course between the two views, staying close to the knowing aspect of *Jabarūt,* while not forgetting Dara Shikoh's description of it as "a state of being in which one sees

1 Schachter-Shalomi, *Gate to the Heart,* 14.
2 Steinsaltz, *The Thirteen Petalled Rose,* 17.
3 "The Compass of Truth" in Kugle, *Sufi Meditation and Contemplation,* 154.

nothing that exists in the human realm or the spiritual realm."[1]

> The breakthrough that marks access to what the Sufis call the *[Jabarūt]* level is triggered off by grasping meaningfulness, which is not based upon an interpretation of existential experience or a search for causality or retrocausality.[2] If consciousness is voided of any perception or conception, being reabsorbed in its ground, which is intelligence, then a meaningfulness is revealed that makes sense of what we could not figure out with our mind. *[...]* That is not the kind of knowledge we acquire but the kind of knowledge that is written right into our intelligence.[3]

THE WORLD OF BEING

Finally, we come to the World of Being. In Hasidism, this is called *Olam ha-Atzilut,* the 'World of Nearness,' being so close to the Divine as to be almost indistinguishable from it.[4] Likewise, in Sufism, it is *'Ālam al-Lāhūt,* the 'World of Divinity,' where there is no separation, everything being merged in the Divine Essence. If the World of Knowing is where the plans are made, or the sketch is drawn, the World of Being is where the pre-formative idea exists. There is no idea there yet, as such, but it is the source of the 'ah-ha!' moment in which you know 'something' which you cannot yet describe. Here, it is as if the whole idea of the unfolding of creation is still in God's mind or belly, as it were; it hasn't yet been 'outer-ed' in any way. This is why it is called the World of Nearness.

In his psychological presentation of the World of Being, Reb

---

1 Ibid.

2 The notion that the effect can occur before the cause, or that the future can effect the present or past.

3 Inayat-Khan, *Awakening Through the Planes,* 49.

4 This interpretation is based on the notion that *Atzilut* is derived from the root, *etzel,* meaning, 'nearness.'

Zalman explains *Atzilut* in terms of intuition derived from the undifferentiated Source:

> The fourth level of reality is *Atzilut,* or 'emanation.'
> This is the world of being, intuition, inner teaching, the
> 'secret' and 'mystery' of *sod,* and the anagogical level of
> interpretation. *Atzilut* is a deep, Divine intuition—a state
> of 'beingness' with God in the soul's aspects of *ḥayyah*
> and *yehidah (yehidah,* actually, is what is 'touching' *Adam
> Kadmon).* It is the source of inspiration *[...].*[1]

According Hasidism and the Kabbalah, *Olam ha-Atzilut* is a World "of such absolute clarity and transparency that no concealment of any essence whatsoever is possible, *[...]* consequently essences do not exhibit any particular separate self at all." For this reason, it is characterized simply as 'Being,' and is seen as nearly identical with Divinity or the Godhead.[2]

From the Sufi perspective, *'Ālam al-Lāhūt* is similarly described as "the uncreated Universe, present and existing in Divine Knowledge. Nothing in it has free will, everything there being subject to absolute dominion."[3] In Pir Vilayat's teaching (because he is using a an expanded schema of Worlds and values), this World of Being is described using the term *Hahūt,* 'is-ness,' or literally, 'he-ness,' instead. Again, he explains the World in terms of consciousness:

> The *[Hahūt]* level is exactly the same as *samadhi.* We have
> lost sight of the multiplicity because we have downplayed
> the multiplicity in unity. All we are aware of is the unity
> behind it all.[4]

---

1 Schachter-Shalomi, *Gate to the Heart,* 14.
2 Steinsaltz, *The Thirteen Petalled Rose,* 22.
3 Ozak, *Adornment of Hearts,* 49, "The World of Dominion comes after the World of Divinity."
4 Inayat-Khan, *Awakening Through the Planes,* 61.

So here we have a sense of undifferentiated consciousness, "where all sense of multiplicity has disappeared. You cannot say you see the unity because you merge into this unity. This is articulated in the words of al-Hallaj: *ana'l haqq!* (I am Truth!)"[1] That it to say, it is experienced by the spiritual adept as union or identity with Divinity.

THE LADDER OF CREATION

Often, these Worlds are described as rungs on "a ladder of intersecting reality-patterns through which we (and all the Universe) ascend and descend, physically and spiritually."[2] Above, I have listed them in order of ascent on the ladder—moving from the world of materiality to the affective world, from the world of the mind to that of undifferentiated being beyond—the journey we all must make back to the Source. But in their descriptions from top to bottom, it is clear that they also describe an evolutionary process of metaphysical unfolding—from the pre-formative idea of creation existing in inchoate Being to the actual idea and plan of creation, from the shaping of the subtle form of it (where everything is plastic and changes are still possible) to the solidified reality of creation as-we-know-it. Or, again, the process might also be compared to the journey from the pot in the potter's mind to the design and drawing of the pot, from the clay spinning on the potter's wheel, shaped by his or her hands, to the finished pot taken baked and dry from the kiln.

THE FOUR SOULS

Interesting as these descriptions might be in themselves, there wouldn't be a lot of point in talking about such metaphysical Worlds if we didn't have a means of experiencing them. Thus, we are also taught about the corresponding Souls of Action, Feeling, Knowing, and Being, through which we are continually

---

1 Vilayat Inayat-Khan, *That Which Transpires Behind That Which Appears: The Experience of Sufism* (New Lebanon, NY: Omega, 1994), 83.
2 Schachter-Shalomi, *Gate to the Heart*, 14.

in contact with these various metaphysical realities.

THE ACTIVE SOUL IN RELATION TO THE BODY

Just as we distinguished between the *matter* of the visible world and its *life,* we also distinguish between the substance of the body—called *guf* or *jasad* (meaning 'flesh' in Hebrew and Arabic, respectively)—and the Active Soul, called *Nefesh* or *Nafs*.[1] This is the vital or animating Soul in the body, its very life and energy. This is the Soul you can feel in a handshake, the glow in a pregnant mother's skin, the very pulse and vibration of all life. It is what is so evidently missing when we look at the body of a friend or loved one who has passed on. It is present in all organic life, from plants to animals to human beings, and perhaps even at lower levels in a way that is difficult to perceive.[2]

It is through the agency of the Active Soul that we do our work in the World of Action. We don't need to say a lot about this, as almost all of our awareness is already given over to it. Nevertheless, it is worth noting that this Active Soul can be 'charged' and 'cultivated' through various kinds of meditative breathing, as well as the breath-coordinated movements of Sufi *dhikr,* Hasidic *davvenen,* Hatha Yoga, and T'ai Chi.[3]

THE FEELING SOUL AND THE ANGELIC REALM

Now the soul through which we do our work in the World of Feeling is called *Ru'aḥ* or *Nafas,* 'wind' or 'spirit' in both Hasidism and Sufism. It is related to wind because it is always in motion. This Feeling Soul is sensitive to and conveyed through presence, quality, attitude, intention, and emotion. While the Active Soul is sensitive to sound, sight, touch, taste, and smell, the Feeling Soul

---

1 When we say *Nafs* here, we are using the word differently than when we talk about *Nafs* as ego.

2 Schachter-Shalomi, *Gate to the Heart,* 9.

3 Ibid. Also discussed in Hazrat Inayat Khan's *Gathas* (Part IV: Pasi Anfas, "The Power of Breath.")

assigns values to these ordinary senses. It is 'stirred' by them in one way or another. It knows whether something has 'heart,' whether music is soulful or vacuous, or whether a prayer is deep or empty. It knows whether there is tension or friendliness in a room, as we have all experienced at one time or another. You see, we forget how much we are in touch with these different Souls all the time, and how much we are actually living through them. We don't think about *why* we know these things; but the esoteric tradition is telling us that we are continually reaching-out with this Soul. And yet, the Feeling Soul is more than just a receiver of information; it is also the means through which we *communicate* presence, qualities, attitudes, intentions, and emotions to the World of Feeling. This is why that World is also called the World of Angels among Sufis.

The Hebrew and Arabic words for angel, *malakh* or *malāk,* both mean 'messenger.' Angels, according to the esoteric theosophical teachings, are not compound beings like us (made up of different elements and filled with complex motivations), but simple essences which convey their own essence as a message.[1] Marshall McLuhan used to say, "the medium is the message," the object is its own message.[2] Well, an angel is very much like that. A feeling of love or hate in a specific context, in a particular moment, becomes an angel that carries that message to the World of Knowing, which receives it and sends back a response in another angelic messenger.[3]

This is actually a description of "Jacob's Ladder." In Genesis 28:12, it says that Jacob dreamed of "a ladder set upon the earth which extended to heaven," on which the angels of God were ascending and descending. This is what angels do—they go up and down. Why do they go up and not just down? Because *we* create angels too. For example, if I'm walking through the park one day and see a little girl on a swing, smiling with delight,

---

1 Steinsaltz, *The Thirteen Petalled Rose,* 8-9.
2 A phrase and concept introduced in his book, *Understanding Media: The Extensions of Man* (New York: Signet Books, 1964).
3 Steinsaltz, *The Thirteen Petalled Rose,* 11-12, 16-17.

and my heart is moved with joy, that moment births an angel. Likewise, if I have a particular kind of frustration with someone at work, or a difficult encounter with my partner, an angel is birthed which conveys that frustration as a message to the higher Worlds. But it's not just emotions. If I have an intention to quit drinking, or an intention to live a life of integrity, an angelic messenger is birthed from that intention too.

Therefore, the types of emotions we feel, and the types of intentions we cultivate, are extremely important. They don't actually stop at the borders of our skin. They travel on through the Feeling Soul to the Knowing Soul which exists in the World of Knowing, and which conveys that message to a Council of Souls or a Heavenly Court which crafts a response, or a 'decree' for us. So we have to take responsibility for our emotions and intentions; we have to cultivate better intentions, a higher quality of feeling, and be careful about what kinds of emotions and intentions we let loose in the Worlds.

The Knowing Soul in the Heavenly Court

The Knowing Soul is called *Neshamah* or *Rūḥ*, 'soul' or 'spirit' in Hebrew and Arabic. As you might expect, it is the Soul that thinks and plans in the World of Knowing, also known as the 'World of Souls.' Now, we have seen that the Feeling Soul is really about conveying emotion and intentions as messages; but where are those messages received, and what is done with them? The World of Knowing is where the archetypes of our personalities, the reflections of our consciousness, our Knowing Souls congregate and conceive together (as a collective) what needs to happen in the World of Action (based on the intentions coming up from our Feeling Souls).[1]

---

1 See Zalman Schachter-Shalomi and Netanel Miles-Yépez, *A Heart Afire: Stories and Teachings of the Early Hasidic Masters* (Philadelphia, PA: Jewish Publication Society, 2009), 58-59, where Reb Zalman and I discuss the Ba'al Shem Tov's report on a spiritual ascent to the Lower *Gan Eden,* where he met with both the "souls of the deceased and the living." In his "Letter on the Four Worlds," the sixth Lubavitcher Rebbe also writes, "All that we know about the Celestial Academy, in which the enlightened souls advance in learned fellowship, the

This is why the Kabbalah also speaks of it in terms of a 'heavenly court,' where judgments are created and decrees are made with regard the World of Action.[1] Moreover, it might also be seen as the place where souls 'rub elbows' and create alliances to make new things, where the soul of Shakespeare may collaborate with the soul of Rumi to create a certain effect in the world.[2]

I personally tend to think of the work of the Knowing Souls as a collective discernment process, a 'feedback mechanism' of the Morphogenic Field, if you will. It collects messages from below, about which it makes a decision, and then sends a response back 'down' into the World of Action. If so many messages of love or hate from the World of Action reach a critical mass in the

order of progression and indoctrination of the newly arrived souls (those who have recently passed on), the abodes of the *tzaddikim* who preside over their followers and direct them to higher attainment, the proclamation, "Make way!" for those great souls who are about to pass over, the order in which the souls of the *tzaddikim* are made welcome [. . .] to *Gan Eden,* the conscious ascents of the souls of Rabbi Yitzhak Luria and the Ba'al Shem Tov [. . .] The whole host of things experienced and seen there, show that these worlds are somehow like this one, the lowest of them, the material world."

1 The notion of the Heavenly Court is based on Daniel 4:17: "This sentence is decreed by the Watchers, the verdict commanded by the Holy Ones." The Heavenly Court is often identified with the Counsel of Souls *(nefashot shel tzaddakim,* lit. 'souls of the righteous') with whom God consulted before creation. The Counsel of Souls is generally thought to be comprised of the souls of the righteous who have ascended to heaven. See Howard Schwartz, *Tree of Souls: The Mythology of Judaism* (New York: Oxford UP, 2004): 160-62, 193-94, 208-09.

2 Likewise, the connections between persons in the World of Action and Souls in the World of Knowing are suggested in various places. The Maggid of Mezritch suggests that when one studies the work of an author, whether living or dead, a kind of link is established between the two souls (Schachter-Shalomi, *A Heart Afire,* 211). In the Kabbalah of the holy Ari, Rabbi Yitzhak Luria, the idea of *ibbur* ('pregnancy') "points to the sharing of a body by different souls that share same soul root," and how a soul above may infuse a person below with a particular inspiration. (Zvi Ish-Shalom, *Radical Death: The Paradoxical Unity of Body, Soul and the Cosmos in Lurianic Kabbalah.* Dissertation: Brandeis University, 2013: 55). In a similar vein, Hazrat Inayat Khan teaches: "If in the plane of the *jinn* a sympathetic link is established between two souls, it continues to exist. In this way it is natural for the spirit of Shakespeare to continue to inspire the Shakespeare personality on earth." (Khan, Hazrat Inayat. *The Sufi Message of Hazrat Inayat Khan: Volume IV,* "The Mind-World" (Surrey, England: Servire Publishing Company, 1978), 273.

World of Knowing, a response of a certain type, meant to act as a corrective in the universe, is created. But it is not a simple, one-to-one, mechanistic response; there is an aggregate or cooperative intelligence shaping the responses, a cosmic balancing system.[1]

The thing to remember about the World of Knowing is that it does not view 'good and evil' the way we do down here. The knowing faculty is, by definition, mentally-oriented and dispassionate, and only looks for healthy, long-term solutions. Thus, when the more elevated, collective consciousness of the Knowing Souls conceive of a corrective for our world, we are often unhappy with the short-term results, which we might even consider 'evil.' There is an interesting anecdote in the Hasidic tradition which precisely illustrates this disparity in perspective:

> Once, Reb Elimelekh saw great trouble approaching the Jewish people and he began to pray very hard for God's help. Later when he was asleep, he saw the Maggid of Mezritch in his dream, and he asked him, "Rebbe, why are you silent? Why don't you cry out against this terrible catastrophe?"
>
> The Maggid answered him, saying, "In Heaven, we do not see any evil—we see only the goodness and the kindness of judgments. You who are on Earth see the good as well as the evil, therefore, you must insist and pray very hard to move the Heavens in these matters."[2]

That is to say, the angel created by our intentions must be 'big' enough to move the Heavenly Court to an action that is as helpful and as satisfying to us in the short-term as it will be in the long-term.

---

1 See Zalman Schachter-Shalomi and Netanel Miles-Yépez, *A Hidden Light: Stories and Teachings of Early HaBaD and Bratzlav Hasidism*, 72, 255-59, where I give a more detailed articulation of this idea and related concepts, and a similar presentation by Reb Zalman and I in *A Heart Afire*, 58-59.
2 Schachter-Shalomi, *A Heart Afire*, 297.

THE INSEPARABLE SOUL OF BEING

Beyond the Knowing Soul is the Being Soul, called *Ḥayyah* and *Idhn* (pronounced, *i-th-in*), 'living essence' and 'permission' in Hasidism and Sufism. This Soul is beyond thinking; it has more to do with intuition and flashes of insight. It is less about process, because it is connected to the World of Being, where everything is intermingled, undifferentiated. There is no real separation between one thing and another. Everything is direct, and thus we get flashes of insight and intuition, making connections that seem spectacular or miraculous.

In the World of Knowing, there is a clear intellectual process. For instance, if I want to start a business, I have to consider a number of factors and tasks. I have to develop the basic idea, consider how I might produce and deliver my product, research how to obtain a business license and pay my quarterly taxes, etc. You put all this information together and go through a process of building an idea into a plan. But with intuition, there is no obvious process.

Think about it this way. Here in the World of Action, many famous discoveries have come about through intuitions: in a flash of insight, John Nash makes a connection between Game Theory and Economics; or August Kekulé makes a connection in a dream between a serpent swallowing its own tail *(ouroboros)* and the arrangement of carbon atoms in Benzene. In our world, there is no apparent or necessary connection between A (representing Game Theory) and C (representing Economics); but, three levels up, in the World of Being, everything is intermingled and intimately connected. That's why an intuition that turns out to be correct seems so amazing; it makes a connection we can't see in the world of separation.

This is one of the most difficult concepts to understand because we are mostly trying to understand it from 'below,' as it were.

LIVING AND WORKING IN THE WORLDS

The reason it is important to know something about these Worlds is because we can be empowered in our spiritual work by remembering that we exist in all of them simultaneously, all the time. For in each successive World we are less affected by the limits of time, space, and matter. Those limits belong to the World of Action. But in the Worlds of Feeling, Knowing and Being, the limits are increasingly irrelevant; so much so, that in Being, there is no 'distance' between anything. What is impossible or improbable because of the limits of the World of Action are possible and can be more easily accomplished in the World of Being. This has important implications for the way we live, the intentions we cultivate, the thoughts we create, and how we respond to our intuition every day—at home and at work, with strangers and friends, family and acquaintances—and especially in how we put it all together in our prayers and meditations.

In the World of Action, there is only so much money you can give to a cause, or so much help you can offer to anyone because of the limits of time, energy, and opportunity. But these limitations fall away in the other Worlds, where you can more freely offer your love, your knowledge, and your insights. In your prayer-life, you can direct all of these to a definite end. Even more importantly, you can work on *yourself* through these Souls. You might ask, 'Am I feeding my body right to give it energy, cultivating and directing my intentions and thoughts in the right way, or responding bravely to my intuitions?' By acting accordingly, we can live more consciously in all Four Worlds, filling-out the most profound dimensions of our being, and doing our best for the health of the planet as a whole.

THE BRIDAL CHAMBER
Returning the Light to the Garden

RABBI TIRZAH FIRESTONE

This teaching is based on the final ma'amar or 'discourse' of the sixth Lubavitcher Rebbe, Rabbi Yosef Yitzhak Schneersohn, called Bati L'Gani, *"I have come into my garden" (Songs 5:1). This discourse is of special significance to Ḥabad-Lubavitcher ḥasidim, as it was received on the day of the Rebbe's* histalkut, *his departure from this world. Thus, it was interpreted as a farewell message by his Ḥasidim (Reb Zalman among them), which, each year on his* yahrzeit, *was interpreted anew by his successor, Rabbi Menachem Mendel Schneerson. Here we have an interpretation of it by one of Reb Zalman's senior students, Rabbi Tirzah Firestone.*

— N.M-Y., editor

THE *MA'AMAR, BATI L'GANI,* was the last discourse written by my rebbe's *rebbe,* Rabbi Yosef Yitzhak Schneersohn, the sixth Lubavitcher Rebbe. In it, the Rebbe demonstrates with rare poignancy the particular potential each of us has for creating an earthly home in which the Divine Presence *(Shekhinah)* can dwell; he illustrates evocatively the mechanism by which we clarify ourselves so as to allow our own unique light to shine into the world. But this light is not merely the happy light of smiles, good moods and personal joy; it is the "hidden light" dwelling in the darkness of existence, a light only revealed through our own deepest efforts.

What follows is a distillation of Reb Yosef Yitzhak's final Torah, illuminated by insights from Rabbi Zalman Schachter-Shalomi's teachings and a few of my own modest annotations. I offer this rendition of *Bati L'Gani* with a prayer that it might release for you living sparks of the universal message of wholeness.

BACK TO THE GARDEN

Bati l'Gani ("I have come into my garden") was written by Reb Yosef Yitzhak early in 1950 with the intention that it be studied in honor of his grandmother, Rebbetzin Rivkah's *yahrzeit,* or death anniversary, on the 10th day of Sh'vat. Thus, it was mailed out to all of the Rebbe's ḥasidim in time for study on this day, which, as it turned out, was to be the day of his own passing.

Receiving their Rebbe's final Torah in the mail on that day, the Ḥasidim intuitively understood the significance of the synchronicity—Reb Yosef Yitzhak was imparting his final message to them—he has entered the garden. "All the efforts for which a soul toils in her lifetime . . . are revealed . . . at the time of her passing."[1] *Bati L'Gani* contained the essence of his life's teaching, and to this day, is studied by Lubavitcher Ḥasidim each year on Reb Yosef Yitzhak's *yahrzeit,* the 10th of Sh'vat.

"I have come into my garden, my sister, my bride," are words that the lover speaks to the beloved in the Song of Songs (5:1). For Reb Yosef Yitzhak, this verse is understood as a metaphor for God's loving relationship with the *Shekhinah,* the Divine Presence dwelling within us, God's people. The return to "my garden" signifies the most intimate meeting place, a return to the "bridal chamber" after a time of separation from the beloved.

In Reb Yosef Yitzhak's understanding, the bridal chamber is also the Holy Sanctuary, the *Beit ha-Mikdash* built by the people in biblical times and to be rebuilt in the Messianic era. My own *rebbe,* Rabbi Zalman Schachter-Shalomi (better known as 'Reb Zalman') would perhaps lay less focus on the literal structure of this intimate meeting place between the Holy One and the

---

1 Free rendering from *Iggeret ha-Kodesh,* letter 28.

Shekhinah, with the understanding that the Bride is us, and the meeting place, the bridal chamber, is the very heart of our being.

Now, we might ask, how is the meeting to take place? It is not enough to be passive; we have to cultivate the ground of meeting so that God can be revealed through us. This is done by tapping our deepest yearnings for holiness and building a structure around these pure intentions.

"Let them make for Me a sanctuary," God says, "and I will dwell within *them.*" This verse from Exodus (25:8) is central to Reb Yosef Yitzhak's interpretation. Notice that God is not saying that the Holy Presence will live within the Sanctuary, but within *them,* the people—for God craves a dwelling-place within each individual. The verse points not only to the need for a spiritual community to build something together, but especially to a formal prerequisite, namely, that each individual create a personal sanctuary within him or herself. As Reb Zalman often counseled, "Do the work of carving-out interior space in which to do the God-work."

Bati L'Gani does not eschew the big questions. It states clearly that the ultimate purpose of creation—seen as an ongoing phenomenon—is for God to have a dwelling-place in the lower worlds.[1] In other words, we, God's creatures, are here to 'host' Divinity on the material plane. And this is the object of all of our spiritual work.

There are various ways of 'languag-ing' this process, the process of preparing ourselves to become a *dirah l'mata,* God's terrestrial residence. I have heard it called by Reb Zalman, the process of becoming a *beit kibbul,* 'a house of receiving.' In a feminine model, the work might be described as the continuous dance of self-surrender; that is, emptying ourselves of our personal preoccupations and desires so that we can better open, hear, and receive God in the inner chambers of the heart.

Working toward the same end with a different emphasis, the Lubavitch lineage of Reb Yosef Yitzhak would have us

---

1 Quoting *Tanhuma,* Parshat B'hukotai, 3.

become servants of the Divine by means of the painstaking work of *it'kaffia,* 'self-mastery,' and *it'hapkha,* transforming or transmuting our physical nature. To me, this is clearly a more rigorous and masculine approach; it speaks of subordinating our human will for God's Will, and turning the world around to see it not through our eyes of desire, but through God's eyes.

In either sensibility, the process is nothing less than alchemy, transforming the dense lead of ego into the gold of God's Presence. Throughout the lineage, from the Alter Rebbe, Shneur Zalman of Liadi to Reb Zalman himself, the master guides have written, taught, and struggled with this alchemical process. Reb Zalman, for one, does not allow his students to push down and pole-vault over their material desires and urges before examining them, discovering their source and message to us. The gravitational pull of the material world must be respected, he says. Instead of denying it, we must work from *within* the system, so to speak, to master each pull on our sensuality, to cherish the limitations of our humanity, which is, after all, also the *Shekhinah.*

THE GREATER LIGHT

The text continues with more metaphors about the Divine and earthly relationship. The Divine Soul, it explains, descends and "enclothes" itself in a body and an animal nature. Through the process of *birrur,* 'sifting' and refining, gaining consciousness and bringing clarity to bear on our situation, we are able to release the Glory of God throughout all the Worlds.

This teaching is fundamental to Hasidic and Lurianic Kabbalah. It is also important to understand that 'Worlds,' *olamot* in Hebrew, shares the same letters as *he-elem,* 'obscurity.' The Worlds, in other words, are where the great Unity is hidden or obscured from the eye. The teaching of the Four Worlds, or dimensions of God's creation, is based upon a passage from Isaiah (43:7)—"All that is called by My Name and for My Glory: I created it, I formed it, and indeed, I made it."

"My Name and My Glory," refer to the state of consciousness

that is so close, yet already slightly separate from the Infinite Unity, the *Ain Sof*. This 'World' so close is called *Atzilut,* from the root which means both 'nearness' from *etzel* and 'separate' from *hatzalah,* meaning 'to separate' or 'save from.' *Atzilut,* the first World, is still a quality of being and light diffusion that is not distinguishable to egoic consciousness. It is the state of union and merger with the Divine, quite different from the other three dimensions referred to with God's verbs. Each of these Worlds receive differing degrees of light, depending upon the absorptive capacity of each one.

B'riyah, the next World, understood to be the beginning of existence, is referred to as the World of Creation. In Reb Zalman's explication, *B'riyah* is the World from which stems faith, knowing, the pure idea. The next state, the World of Formation, has a still more obscured light. Known in Hebrew as *Yetzirah,* it is the state of consciousness in which we are already separate entities with the yearning to be whole, reunited. Here lies feeling, relationship, love and pain. Finally, the last verb in the verse ("I made it") applies to the World of Making or Action, known in Hebrew as *Assiyah.* Here is the 'World' of our deeds, where the drama of physical life, in all its particulars, takes place. Here, the brilliant light of the *Ain Sof* is most obscure, and it is here that all spiritual intention must finally be translated into what is done.

But, there is another kind of light, a light that rises from below, elicited and drawn into the world through our labors. This light, called *sovev kol almin,* encompasses all the worlds without distinguishing this level or that. It is a light that is absorbed through our own efforts and is emitted to the Worlds through the work of *birrur,* 'sifting,' the work of Self which is called 'divine service': the chafing to discern who we are and what we must become, what within us is essential and what will pass away. It is the work of sitting with ourselves, restraining our urges, mastering our words and actions, and dedicating ourselves again and again and again to that which is Eternal.

In the Zohar's admittedly dualistic language, it is described in the highest manner: "When the *sitra ahra* (literally, 'Other Side,' the cosmic side opposing holiness) is subdued, the glory of God rises throughout all the worlds." The Zohar is telling us that there are different forms of light, and the greatest kind is emitted through the hard labor of our divine service, when we succeed in transmuting the forces of our inner darkness into light. This is the most glorious light, for it is born of the darkness itself. As the Zohar so lucidly teaches: ". . . there is no good except that which comes from evil; and through this good His glory is exalted, and this is perfect worship."[1]

WOOD WITH A TWIST

The transformation of darkness into light was made possible, in the ancient and sacred technology, by means of the work and worship at the Sanctuary in the Holy Temple. One of the primary modes of worship there was the bringing of sacrifices. Accompanied by the Priests' and Levites' hymns and music, this was a national ritual that served a spiritual need.

For Reb Yosef Yitzhak, the meaning of sacrifice was based upon the verse, "A person who brings from you an offering (korban) to God, from cattle, herd or flocks, shall you bring your offering . . ." This awkward syntax is not accidental. The seemingly extraneous words "from you," point to the central spiritual issue: sacrifice (korban) in the work of the individual soul is nothing if it is not a "bringing from you" the gift of our individual selves.[2] And although we terminated the practice of sacrifice long ago, sacrifice remains a critical part of our spiritual work. Today it is not actual animals that we must surrender to God, but the 'animal' within. This is not to disparage the Earth's wild kingdom, but simply refers to our baser instincts, appetites and territorial drives, which, if left unbridled, can cause immense harm. This, too, is part of the process of self-emptying, preparing the Garden for the sacred meeting.

1 Zohar II, 184a.
2 The actual translation of the word korban is 'drawing near to God.'

Remember that the central service of the Sanctuary was the conversion of darkness into light. By means of sacrifice and the interior space it opened within the person offering it, God's sparks were freed to radiate from the Sanctuary into the whole world.

But there is a twist. In the Mishnah, the sanctuary had to be built of *shittim* or acacia wood. Ironically, Reb Yosef Yitzhak explains, it was *shittim* wood that had to be used because it is associated with (by letters, and hence, divine energy) *Shin-Tet-Heh,* the letters for 'deviation,' and *Shin-Tet-Vav-Tav,* the letters of the word for 'foolishness.' The same root appears again in the name of the place, Shittim, where the Israelites encamped on their way out of Egypt, and where they were lured into bawdy and licentious activities. Deviance, foolishness, unholy sexuality . . . how strange to craft an altar and sanctuary from the likes of these!

Herein lies an essential teaching about the power of unreason and the need for the tension between opposites. Righteousness is nothing at all without the tension of its opposite, the free choice to commit all manner of folly and lewdness. This paradox of the spiritual path is reiterated throughout the rabbinic texts with the central teaching that the flawless person cannot compare with the one who has deviated and brought him or herself back to awareness.

Beware the devotee who has never fallen off the path! The very fiber of the Sanctuary is laughing at us here, reminding us that no Union can be achieved without a tension of opposites. Lest we get too self-righteous or pompous in our efforts, we are chided to remember that without deviance from the path, there is no path at all; without poor judgments deeply experienced, good judgment cannot be deeply learned. The Sanctuary, symbol of our truest service and ultimately, our meeting place with God, is built of *shittim* wood. It requires that we build on, and build with our own wholly necessary, 'unholy' energies of folly.

And In The End

"... *Feast, friends! And drink until you are drunk with love!*" So ends the passage of Reb Yosef Yitzhak's explication with an invitation to loosen the tight constraints of our reason and give ourselves over to the dance of merriment, for the heart has long ago surrendered the struggle to understand in favor of love.

Bati L'Gani: God has entered the Garden, and there, in the wedding chamber, awaits you and I. We are the "sister," we are the "bride." Every one of us participates in Her, the *Shekhinah;* the great circle-dance humanity forms, itself constitutes the Beloved, the *Anima Mundi,* the World Soul.

The wedding dance requires just one thing: that each of us encounter the cavernous darkness of our own individual life-experience and find a way to kindle the candle of our clarity in that obscuring night. It may take a million candles, millions of kindlings! But there is surely no act more godly than this effort, no gesture more beloved of God than our doings and misdoings, our meetings and missed meetings, our pure yearnings and feeble blunderings in sincere effort. Our efforts bring us, in the end, to encounter our self, the only Self, to the meeting place where all opposites are softened into One. Then the spark catches, and is breathed into flame. And the wedding begins.

THE TEACHINGS OF
MENACHEM MENDEL SCHNEERSON
OF LUBAVITCH

WHEN WILL THE WEDDING TAKE PLACE?
A Little Known Discourse of the Seventh Lubavitcher Rebbe

RABBI SHAUL MAGID

EDITOR'S INTRODUCTION

In September of 1940, Zalman Schachter, just 16 years old, was released from a French internment camp and came to Marseilles to await passage to America with his family. While there, he attended a seudah shlishit (third meal) one Shabbat, which was led by Reb Shneur Zalman Schneersohn, a direct descendant of Reb Shneur Zalman of Liadi. Afterward, he asked if he might walk the rabbi home. This is Reb Zalman's own account:

He agreed, and I walked him toward the Hotel de Monde and told him about our needs. I said, "Look, there are a number of us here, and all day long we have nothing to do but twiddle our thumbs. We're refugees—we cannot work— and we need something to do. It would be wonderful if we could have someone who would come and teach us?" So he hired Hayyim Meir Zilberstein, the *moreh shiur* from the *yeshiva* in Heide to come and be our teacher.

We met in the Rue de Convalescents, and for half a day we learned Talmud, and began our study of the Tractate

Ketubot (marriage contracts). One day, Reb Shneur Zalman comes by to check on us and says, "I can't be with you for the Tu B'Shvat holiday, but I'll send a guest to talk to you in my place." Then he gave us money to buy some schnapps and fruit for our *farbrengen* (gathering) and walked out.

Some weeks before this, young Zalman had seen a curious figure around the synagogue. He wore a grey suit and a fedora, but he also had a beard which was an uncommon combination in those days. Ḥasidim wore beards and black suits, while non-Ḥasidim were clean-shaven and dressed in grey suits. Nevertheless, here was a man in both. Finally, he came to terms with this incongruity after overhearing the man studying in perfect French and Arabic with a Moroccan scholar—"Obviously," he thought, "he's Moroccan." Reb Zalman continued his story:

The night of the *farbrengen,* we're all sitting around and singing *niggunim,* when the guest speaker arrives—it was "the Moroccan" in his grey suit and hat! And to my growing amazement, he greets us in Yiddish, *"Gut yontif!"* and says *"L'ḥayyim!"* to us, and we replied, *L'ḥayyim v'livrakha,* "to life and blessing," establishing our field of fellowship in which spiritual teaching could begin to take root.

He sat down at the head of the table and I leaned forward to get a good look at him. He asked, "What are you learning here?" So, I say, "We are learning *Ketubos.*" He replied, *"L'ḥayyim!"* over a small glass of schnapps and began an extemporaneous discourse on that talmudic portion.

When he came to the end, he started to cough, which was a cover for the fact that he had begun to cry. He had touched on some sensitive issues in our past that were palpable in our present. He spoke about raising the sparks of holiness buried in the shells of our ignorance as a prelude to the coming of the Messiah and lamented, as we all did, that the Messiah had not yet come.

Not one of us was unaffected—we were all children of the Holocaust years, not knowing what our fate would be, and dreaming of redemption.

It was quiet for a moment.

Finally, he recovered, and began to lead us in some *niggunim*. He then gave a little talk on Tu B'Shvat and departed. I was blown away by him. . . . I asked someone, "Who was that man?" and was told, "Rabbi Schneerson from Nizza (Nice), near the Italian border." I had never heard of him.[1]

What follows is Reb Zalman's remembrance of that discourse by "the Moroccan," who turned out to be Rabbi Menachem Mendel Schneerson who, just ten years later, would become the seventh Lubavitcher Rebbe. As far as I know, this teaching of Reb Menachem Mendel exists in no other account, being resident only in Reb Zalman's memory from that Tu B'Shvat in 1941. Over the years, he repeated it for his own learning, but rarely as a teaching. Nevertheless, in 2004, he gave it over to this editor in both the original and English.[2] What follows is an edited version of the transcript with a commentary by the well-known scholar of Hasidism and modern Jewish thought, Shaul Magid.

— N.M-Y., editor

"IT IS SO LATE ON FRIDAY AFTERNOON . . ."

" 'A VIRGIN IS BETROTHED on the fourth day (Thursday).' Why do the sages say that she is married only on the fourth day? Because, if it is discovered that she is not a virgin, her husband can approach the *Beit Din*, which meets on the fifth day, and make his claim that she is not a virgin.[3]

---

1 These quotes are from an unpublished manuscript by Zalman Schachter-Shalomi and Netanel Miles-Yépez.

2 On March 22nd, 2004, in Reb Zalman's home in Boulder, Colorado. It was then shared with the author, who transcribed and edited it.

3 Mishnah, Ketubot 1:1. "A virgin is married on the fourth day [of the week] and a widow on the fifth day, for the *Beit Din* sit in the town twice a week—on the second day and on the fifth day. If a husband has a claim to the virginity [of his bride] he could go nearly [on the fifth day] to the *Beit Din*."

"Why is it that one does not marry on Sunday given that the *Beit Din* also sits in judgment on the second day (Monday)? This is because the women must have three days to prepare for the wedding.[1]

"Now, who is the virgin? Israel is the virgin. Who is the husband? God is the husband.[2]

"There are numerous dimensions of the Jewish marriage ceremony that require consideration here. The first is the engagement *(tena'im),* the commitment of the intent to marry. The second is the betrothal, enacted with the offering of the ring from the bridegroom to the bride. The third and final phase is the marriage ceremony, including the recitation of the *ketubah* and the seven blessings.[3]

"The woman spoken of in this *mishnah* is one who is in the final stage of the marital process, the marriage ceremony. The final stage of the marriage here represents the coming of the Messiah. Hence, it is on the fourth day because the Rabbis said, "There are three periods of history—the first two thousand years consist of confusion *(tohu),* the second two thousand consist of Torah, and the third two thousand are the era of Messiah."[4]

"The culmination of the first four thousand years (the first two

---

1 Talmud, Ketubot 2b. The language of the Talmud is somewhat different. It states that she and/or her family need three days (after *Shabbat)* to prepare the meal for the wedding.

2 See R. Shneur Zalman of Liadi, *"Drush 'al Ha-Hatuna,"* in *Tefillah m'Kol Ha-Shana* (Brooklyn, 1981), p. 125a/b where he makes this analogy. It seems likely that R. Schneerson is basing himself on this homily.

3 See Mishnah, Kiddushin 1:1. Cf. b.*T Ketubot* 7b.

4 See b.*T. Sanhedrin* 97a and *Avodah Zara* 9a. It appears R. Schneerson's statement here relates directly to the dictum in b.*T. Sanhedrin* 99a. "Abimi the son of R. Abbahu learned: The days of the Messiah shall be seven thousand years, as it is written, *And as the bridegroom rejoiced over the bride, so shall God rejoice over you.* (Isaiah 62:5)." The use of Isaiah's image of marriage and the era of redemption is employed in the Abimi's statement but it is never made explicit what the seven thousand year mark has to do with the marriage metaphor. R. Schneerson fills in that lacuna by suggesting that the tripartite ceremony of marriage correlates to the six thousand years before the final part of the redemptive era that is inaugurated in the beginning of the seven thousandth year.

periods of history) on the fourth day should be the beginning of the messianic era. The engagement was at the moment of creation, as it is written [in Midrash], "God made an oath *(tana'a hatana)* with creation."[1] That oath, that contract, was Torah. If Israel keeps the Torah, the world will continue to exist—if Israel rejects the Torah, the purpose for existence becomes void.

"The conditions (for the Messiah) were thus instituted at creation. This moment represents the *tena'im,* or the first stage of the marriage ceremony that expresses the intent to marry. When was the betrothal, or the second stage? This was the time of the Torah (Sinai) *'et yom hatunato* (Wearing the crown that his mother gave him [King Solomon] on his wedding day, on the day of his bliss).[2] Come out and see King Solomon, "Solomon, a king who embodies peace *(sh'ha-shalom shelo),*"[3] this would have been at Sinai, after the conclusion of the two thousand years of *tohu* (chaos). At that time God would have given the ring [to Israel]. And what was the ring? The ring was the *mitzvot,* as we say *asher kidashanu b'mitzvitav* (that God would enact *kiddushin* with Israel through the *mitzvot).*

"So, now we can understand why the Rabbis teach that the bride must have three days in order to make herself ready for the wedding. We understand this by employing the kabbalistic notion that sets the conditions for creation. Before the beginning

---

1 Genesis Raba 5:4. "Said Rabbi Yohanan, God made an oath with the sea [at creation] that it should divide before Israel, as it is written, *And the sea returned to its strength* (Exodus 14:27). R. Jeremiah son of Eliezer said: Not with the sea alone did God make an oath but with everything that was created in the six days of creation, as it is written, *I, even My hands have stretched out the heavens, and all their host have I commanded.* (Isaiah 65:12). The connection between this midrash and the point being made here is unclear. Perhaps it means the following: The oath God makes with the sea, or all of creation, concerns nature agreeing to protect Israel. However this protection is contingent upon another oath God makes with Israel, that is, Torah. If Israel does not live by its oath, nature does not have to live by its oath and thus nature becomes a destructive force and not a protection for Israel.
2 Song of Songs 3:11.
3 See Midrash Zuta to Song of Songs, 3; Yalkut Shemoni to Exodus, 25:369; and Yalkut Shemoni to Song of Songs, 3.

of creation, kabbalists argue there was 'a rupture of the vessels,' *shvirat ha-kelim,* and the sparks that were dispersed through that rupture were lodged in all dimensions of material and spiritual existence.[1] When one does something good in the world, some of those lost sparks are raised and returned to their origin. In the kabbalistic imagination, this process of 'raising the sparks' is the foundation of all redemptive activity.

"It is written that before Israel left Egypt there were 288 sparks that were lost. 202 were elevated to their source when we left Egypt, as it is written *the* erev rav *went up with them* (Exodus 12:38). RB *(rav)* = 202.[2] The *erev rav* elevated 202 sparks, leaving 86 sparks still lodged in creation. The *gematria* of *elohim* is 86.[3] Thus, the remainder are sparks of divine judgment *(gevurah).*[4]

"If we would have merited divine mercy through our behavior, we would have merited the Messiah at that time, i.e., with the Exodus and Sinai. This is captured in the verse in Jeremiah, I will always remember the days after you walked after me in the desert, during the wedding.[5] But, as we know, Israel sinned.

"Now, there are sins that are unintentional *(sho'geg),* likened to a widow who has no control over the fact that her husband dies. If Israel would have been like a widow, the Talmud teaches that the widow can marry on the fifth day. The fifth day would have been the year five thousand. Why can the widow marry on the fifth day?[6] Because on the fifth day the fishes were created

---

1 See *Eitz Ḥayyim* (Warsaw, 1891, r.p. Jerusalem, 1975), 9:1-8, pp. 40a-47b.

2 On the 288 sparks that were scattered after *shvirat ha-kelim,* see *Eitz Ḥayyim* 18:1-6, pp. 85c-89d. In terms of the *erev rav* as constituting 202 of those sparks I have not found a source in Lurianic *kabbalah.* For a source that equates the *erev rav* with speaks more generally, see *Eitz Ḥayyim* 32:2, pp. 35d, 36a.

3 Reb Zalman notes in his re-telling of the homily that R. Schneerson did not give over the connection between the 86 remaining sparks and the *gematria* of *elohim.*

4 This is because in the Zohar and theosophic *kabbalah* more generally, the divine name *elohim* corresponds to the manifestation of divine judgment or severity.

5 I have note been able to locate the verse in Jeremiah to which this refers.

6 Mishnah, Ketubot 1:1.

and God said to them, *be fertile, increase and fill the waters of the sea* (Genesis 1:22).

"That blessing would have been our blessing if we had deserved it. Intentional sins *(ma'zid)* are likened to a divorce. In our metaphor, this is the case where the husband (God) found a blemish in her (Israel). That is, she was not a virgin. When does a divorcee get married? She marries on the sixth day so she can merit the blessing of humans, *be fruitful and multiply* (Genesis 1:28)[1] . . . *[Here, R. Schneerson coughed]* It is already so late on Friday (afternoon), when will the wedding take place?"

THE RIGHT WEDDING

The context, and more pointedly . . . the anguish of this homily is captured in the final sentence, "it is already so late on Friday (afternoon), when will the wedding take place?" Expanding the metaphor of marriage as a reflection of Israel's covenant with God, a covenant that contains the Messiah as its ultimate promise, R. Menachem Mendel allows himself to consider the worst-case scenario. That is, that Israel is likened to a divorced wife, abandoned by her husband because she was not unworthy

---

1 I have not found an explicit reference in rabbinic or halakhic literature that stipulates a divorcee should or can marry on the sixth day. In *Tosefta Ketubot* 1:1 we read that a virgin should not be married on the sixth day lest her husband cause a wound on *Shabbat* by penetrating her hymen. This would not apply to a divorcee but it would also not apply to a widow. In *Shulḥan Arukh "Even Ha-Ezer"* 64:3 we read that no Jewish wedding should take place on Friday lest one come to desecrate the *Shabbat* in preparation or in cleaning up from the meal *(tikkun ha-se'udah)*. However, it continues, "There are those who are lenient and there is a custom to have weddings on *Erev Shabbat* as long as the preparation for the meal begins three days in advance." R. Joseph Karo makes no distinction here between a virgin, a widow or a divorcee and apparently does not consider the Tosefta's concern about a wound binding. None of the commentaries on this comment make any substantive remark relevant to our concern. As far as I can tell, the comment about a divorcee getting married on Friday has no basis in halakhic discourse.

of his companionship.[1]

The divorcee in this case embodies the notion of intentional sin. This stands in opposition to the widow, whose status is beyond her control, and even the non-virgin who poses as a virgin; her sin is not against her husband per se but simply an act of deception. It is the divorcee who is the guiltiest of all women in this metaphor. And yet, even she deserves to be re-covenanted.[2] Her sin is diminished because she lives in a broken world (a world after the rupture of the vessels and after the initial elevation of the 202 sparks through the *erev rav*). Mired in a world of judgment without mercy, she stands, even in her guilt, ready for her moment of betrothal, expecting the same promise of intimacy as the virgin.

The widow is guiltless, a victim of misfortune. Thus, she can marry on a day when the fish, who, immersed in water (or Torah), are blessed with fertility. The fifth day is the day of *Matan Torah*, the day when Torah (as water) engulfs the world to liberate the anguish of the widow. But Israel is not a widow—her sins are premeditated and intentional. Thus she cannot survive in the waters of Torah, and must breathe the air that contains the fallen sparks of creation in need of repair. Here lies the opportunity, but also the pain. Human beings must wait until the end to be created, and Israel must wait until the end to be redeemed. Friday, the day that holds the promise of reconciliation, the day when even the divorcee stands awaiting the return of her spouse, shows itself to be black and lifeless.

European Jewry is in ashes, countless righteous and innocent souls have perished, and millions of Jewish children will never stand at their wedding canopy. And yet, and yet . . . at least two people remain standing—one, the scion of a Hasidic dynasty, and the other, a young devotee. One speaks and the other listens,

---

1 This motif appears numerous times in the Prophets. See, for example Jeremiah 3:20. *Instead, you have broken faith with Me, as a woman breaks faith with a lover, O House of Israel—declares the Lord.*

2 The sages even consider a husband re-marrying his divorced wife as a noble act under certain circumstances. See Mishnah, Gittin, 4.

one leads a dynasty into the next era and passed from the earth expectant, while the other continues to tell the story of the forlorn divorcee who stands and wonders . . . "it is so late Friday afternoon, where is my beloved?"

It is as if R. Menachem Mendel is saying, "I have searched the depths of the Torah, and, even according to the worst case scenario, I deserve you. Nevertheless, all I see is a wasteland—there is no mountain to ascend, no wedding to prepare, no reconciliation in sight!" I read these as the thoughts of a man, once hopeful, on the verge of despair, looking for something to believe in, hoping to find some ray of light in his erudition . . . but coming up short. He has not yet reached the radical submission R. Kalonymous Kalman Shapira of Piasetzno had reached recorded in his 'Aish Kodesh in the months following the Great Deportation before he too would become a victim of the Holocaust. The words of R. Kalonymous Kalman were the words of one who had no more tears to shed, one who could only wait and wonder, and wonder whether it is worth the wait. R. Menachem Mendel's words are the words of one still fighting on this side life, wondering about the blessing of surviving . . . and waiting.

The cough that precedes the final sentence is striking. Reb Zalman tells us that this was R. Menachem Mendel's way of covering for his tears. He had become choked up, his air blocked by the words he had allowed himself to utter? There is more R. Menachem Mendel wants to say, it seems, but the cough interrupts, silencing a renewed flow of words. Perhaps the cough tells us more than all the words, the struggle for breath; perhaps that is what one had to do in Marseilles, to continue trying to breathe, never quite knowing how much air was left.

This is not a homily that inspires, and certainly not one that has an answer. Rather, it is, in its frailty, a cough—discomforting and pained. In some way, this reflects the first chapter of tractate *Ketubot.*

One would think the first rabbinic discourse on marriage should be joyous. In fact, it is largely about failure and deception. 'What if I don't get what I expect? What if my spouse deceives me? What if this covenant called marriage is really a sham?' Who could blame someone standing on the precipice of life and death, hope and despair, not to have similar thoughts about God's covenant with Israel? And yet, even though the hour is late, he waits ... and we listen.

Then there is the student, Reb Zalman, the one who tells the story; like the teacher, he survives the catastrophe and continues to struggle with the question. And in his struggle he continues on, saying, "if it is Friday afternoon, however late, I must prepare for *Shabbos.*" He wonders, "Maybe there is something else I can do to prepare for *Shabbos?*" He runs to the *mikveh* in his new homeland, America, passing all the alienated and apathetic refugees (most of whom don't even know they are survivors! survivors of what?). And he finds himself, among other locals, in the Haight Ashbury district, among the hippies and activists fighting truth to power. "It is still Friday afternoon, yes, and *Shabbos* is coming, maybe, but these poor souls don't even realize what has happened, what is supposed to be happening."

Both the student and the teacher continue to prepare for *Shabbos.* But, as time goes on, their preparations look different. The teacher continues to believe that this Friday afternoon is like any other. Everything has changed, and nothing has changed.

His student sees another world. Everything has changed means *everything* has changed! And yet, it is still Friday afternoon (how can that change?), and we must continue to prepare for *Shabbos.* Still, he ponders again . . . "maybe Friday afternoon seems like forever because we are not preparing in the right way. Maybe the problem is in our preparation, and not in our past sins. Maybe we remain unmarried because we are preparing for the wrong wedding!? *Gevalt!* The *Shoah* didn't just change the Jews—it changed the whole world! To be a Jew in the world means something else—something more! Preparing for *Shabbos* now doesn't only mean closing oneself off from the world, but inviting the whole world to the wedding! The paradigm shift has occurred, Gaian consciousness has risen; the Jews remain broken, but new preparations for the global Shabbos are intensifying and the Jews must play a crucial role!"

There is a chilling torah I once heard from Reb Shlomo Carlebach, a comrade-in-arms of Reb Zalman. Talking about Rabbi Yohanan ben Zakkai who abandoned the Temple for Yavneh before the destruction, the one who inaugurated the "new" Judaism of the Mishnah, Reb Shlomo said, "How can it be that God destroyed the Jews of Europe with all that torah and sacred teaching? Maybe it was precisely because, as holy as it was, that *torah* wasn't good enough—maybe we need a new *torah*." He then began singing the psalm, *shiur l'Ha-Shem, shir ḥadash* ("sing a new song to God")!

This homily has survived in Reb Zalman's heart, and exists for us only because he has chosen to re-tell it, again and again, in many different ways. And he re-tells it because it is still alive. But how is it alive? Where does it point us? As I read it, it suggests that we must re-consider our "intentional sins," re-consider the very notion of intentional sin, as well as its content. Are they just sins against God? Are they also against the world? Have we abandoned the world for the sake of our wedding? Has Torah become a tool of exclusion? Has *ethnos* effaced *theos*? Are we coughing because we refuse to breath the air around us, the scent of other peoples, believing they are defiled? Are we allowing the air we breathe to become defiled with the poison of human waste?

Perhaps Reb Zalman's re-telling of the homily is subverting it. Yes, yes, it is still Friday afternoon and the time moves slow. But maybe it is we who are holding back the arms of the clock? Perhaps it is we who are inadvertently contributing to our own anguish at the excruciatingly slow passage of time. Perhaps revising the *ketubah* nullifies the writ of divorce? And yet . . . yet . . . perhaps not. How are we to know? Of course, we cannot—all we can do is live 'as if' it is Friday afternoon. All we can do is look around us and respond to what we think is demanded of us, fearlessly, and with joy. All we can do is prepare for *Shabbos* as we would want *Shabbos* to be. Perhaps Friday afternoon is not preparing for *Shabbos* at all—perhaps it is making *Shabbos* happen, creating the conditions for *Shabbos!*

A *rebbe* provides lenses for his or her Ḥasidim to allow us to see that which we saw before, only see it differently. It is then up to us to interpret that new vision. These are the lenses Reb Zalman has bequeathed us, and for that, we, and subsequent generations, owe him an eternal debt of gratitude.

GOING HOME AGAIN
The True Meaning of T'shuvah

PASTOR EMANUEL GOLDMANN

This meditation is based on teaching given by the seventh Lubavitcher Rebbe, Rabbi Menachem Mendel Schneerson, at a gathering on the 7th day of Tishri, 5713 (1952) during the ten days of t'shuvah. It is interpreted here by Pastor Emanuel Goldmann, a German Christian student of Reb Zalman, who studied Hasidic texts with him, and whom Reb Zalman described as a "Hasidic Lutheran."

— N.M-Y., editor

THERE IS A MOST SIGNIFICANT DIFFERENCE
Between the meaning and implications
Of the Hebrew, 't'shuvah,' and it's
English equivalent, 'repentance.'

Repentance suggests regret,
Remorse, contrition, and a
Host of penitential disciplines.
It implies an abrogation of the past
(Or, at least, recent parts of it),
A turning away from a deficient,
Sinful path or practice a person has
Followed up to that moment,
To go in a new direction.
Thus, the sin, the negativity,

The error, acknowledged as such,
Become the dominant points
Of reference in 'repentance.'

How different
The perspective
Opened by 't'shuvah'!
T'shuvah, at its root and core,
Means re-turn, coming home.
And though it does imply the
Necessity of correcting one's course,
All such corrections are determined
And qualified by a premise indicated
By that very word, t'shuvah, 'return':
Re-turn, obviously, refers to a place
Where one has been before,
Or to a mode of being
Touched in the past,
Still within reach
Whatever may have
Happened since.

T'shuvah
Claims and proclaims
An indelible belonging,
An inalienable connectedness
To a Source, which —
Even though abandoned —
Remains there, waiting,
Inviting a return,
Calling for the renewal of life,
Cleansed and nourished
By the living waters of the source.
T'shuvah grows out of an experience
Deeply ingrained in the Torah-infused mind:

Preceding and calling forth the individual's existence,
The Reality of the Covenant established by G-d
Truly is the Root and Source, to which,
All *t'shuvah*-efforts are related.
The Bow of the Covenant
Encompasses all that is.

The endowment
And encouragement
Implied in '*Tzelem Elokim*,'
The very image of G-d,
Is never really annulled by sin.
No level is there in a human's existence
That is beyond the scope of G-d's
Promise and command.
However far a person may have strayed,
However great one's own distance
From G-d's original intent —
There is no 'point of no return.'
Wherever I am, what is commanded of me,
Here and now, is not to arrive at a distant goal,
But to take the one . . . first step of *t'shuvah*, 're-turn,'
That is possible and due right now.
The call to take this first step,
Fragmentary though it may be,
Is G-d's command for me
In the here and now:
No less a *mitzvah* than
Any other commandment could be.
And since being *metzuweh*, 'commanded' —
According to the witness of Jewish experience —
Means 'being bound' to G-d,
Taking the *mitzvah* of re-turning seriously
Is acknowledging this existing bond
And beginning the process of allowing G-d

To re-shape us according to Hir Blessed Will.[1]*
Thus, even in the first small step of *t'shuvah*
One opens oneself to the Kingdom of G-d,
And consciously draws on the Root and Source
Of one's own and of all being.

No future incarnation
Could possibly add to
The essential promise and task
Of such living in the Presence of the Living G-d,
Taking on the yoke of the Kingdom of Heaven.
Therefore, whoever does *t'shuvah*,
Actually anticipates the essence
Of all lives and worlds to come.

What a Blessing
To have become attuned
To the process of living *t'shuvah*
By a teacher as inspiring and compassionate
As Reb Meshullam Zalman Schachter-Shalomi Ha'Kohen.
"Zikhrono liv'rakha le'hayyei ha'Olam ha'Ba — Amen!"

---

1 The use of Hir is an homage to Reb Zalman who, in the 1980s was experimenting with a gender-neutral pronoun for God. — N.M-Y., editor

SEARCHIN'
The Geologist of the Soul

MATISYAHU MILLER

The following piece is a personal and poetic exploration of a mashal *or parable of the seventh Lubavitcher Rebbe, Rabbi Menachem Mendel Schneerson, reported by Reb Zalman, who heard it directly from the Rebbe (see Appendices). When the Jewish singer-songwriter, Matisyahu, was working on his album,* Spark Seeker *(2012), he contacted Reb Zalman and asked him to his studio to record selected teachings that might inspire songs and be sampled in them. Thus, the song, "Searchin," on the continual longing and search for God, includes samples of Reb Zalman giving over the "geologist of the soul" mashal of the Rebbe.[1]**

— N.M-Y., editor

"IN THE EARTH,
There are so many
Wonderful treasures.
And if you know
Where to dig,
You will find gold
And diamonds,
All kinds of treasures.

---

1 This version is an amalgam of the lyrics as sung on *Spark Seeker* (2012) and *Spark Seeker: Acoustic Sessions* (2013).

But if you don't know
Where to dig,
All you'll find is
Rocks and dirt.
He can show you
Where to dig,
And what to dig for,
But the digging
You must do yourself,
The digging you
Must do yourself."

Let go
Of what ya' know,
Return to the land
Of the rainbow,
Where the sun hang low,
And the wind does blow,
And the time it moves so slow,
Creeps and go through the window,
Return to the land where the wild may roam,
And the buffalo go, yeah, the buffalo go,
Where the wild may roam and *ehh . . .*

Across the countryside, search far and wide,
Dig until I reach upon the other side,
Streams and the rivers and the oceans and the seas
And I swim with the fishes down deep.

I've been searchin' for you,
I've been searchin' far and wide,
I've been searchin' for you
All my life, my life.

I've been searchin' for you,
I've been searchin' far and wide,
I've been searchin' for you
All my life, my life,
My life.

Lift your eyes upon the hillside,
Sunrise and I fight to see through the lies,
Creep upon the hills, oh I'm oh so high,
When I run upon the heights feelin' oh so right,
Run upon the land and I'm kickin' up sand,
When I stand and deliver my plan,
Won't you please back down,
Or get slammed to the ground,
When my sound strike thunder,
While you pillage and plunder,
Now you wonder why you going under,
Got yourself on the run from the number one
That you can't run from,
Your spirit fades,
You feel hunger,
Hunger.

I've been searchin' for you,
I've been searchin' far and wide,
I've been searchin' for you
All my life, my life.

I've been searchin' for you,
I've been searchin' far and wide,
I've been searchin' for you
All my life, my life,
My life.

"In the Earth,
There are so many
Wonderful treasures.
And if you know

Where to dig,
You will find gold
And diamonds . . .
Diamonds . . .
Diamonds."

I've been searchin' for you,
I've been searchin' far and wide,
I've been searchin' for you
All my life, my life.

I've been searchin' for you,
I've been searchin' far and wide,
I've been searchin' for you
All my life, my life,
My life.

"In the Earth,
There are so many
Wonderful treasures.
And if you know
Where to dig,
You will find gold
And diamonds,
And silver —
All kinds of treasures.

But if you don't know
Where to dig,
All you'll find is
Rocks and dirt.
A rebbe *is the*
Geologist of the soul —
He can show you
Where to dig,
And what to dig for,
But the digging
You must do yourself,
The digging you
Must do yourself."

TEACHING TORAH
A Light Unto the Denominations

RABBI BAHIR DAVIS

This teaching is inspired by an encounter Reb Zalman witnessed between the seventh Lubavitcher Rebbe, Rabbi Menachem Mendel Schneerson, and a Reform rabbi in the late 1950s or early 1960s. Bahir Davis is a Reform trained rabbi from a family of Reform rabbis who later became a personal student of Reb Zalman.

— N.M-Y., editor

THERE IS A STORY my Rebbe, Rabbi Zalman Schachter-Shalomi tells of his own Rebbe that I find particularly useful when it comes to the question of "Who is Jew?" Reb Zalman tells it like this:

As a Hillel director, I used to attend various conferences with other Hillel directors and occasionally traveled with them. And often, when I would return to New York to see the Rebbe, another Hillel director would come with me, and I would ask them, "Would you like to have an audience with the Rebbe?" And most of the time they were interested.

I remember one such occasion when I went in with a friend who was a Reform rabbi. In the course of conversation, he said to the Rebbe, "Should I become Orthodox, then?" And the Rebbe said, "No, you are needed where you are. Just get out there and teach! And you should say to me, 'Hey, Schneerson! What are you doing just sitting behind your desk? You should get out there, too!'"[1]

---

1 A story told by Rabbi Zalman Schachter-Shalomi to the editor of this volume.

Now, Reb Menachem Mendel Schneerson, the seventh Lubavitcher Rebbe, was among the most revered of Orthodox Jewish teachers (not to mention, one of the great figures of modern Judaism); but, nevertheless, here he is legitimizing a Reform rabbi! Well, as a Reform trained rabbi from a family of staunch Reform rabbis, I am more than a little impressed by this. But, more than that, he seems to be saying that *hasidut* is not the possession of a denomination, but rather a tool for all those who out there teaching Torah! Hearing this, I am reminded of how the three rebbes in my life have taught and still teach Torah.

RABBI ABRAHAM CRONBACH
(FEBRUARY 16TH, 1882 - AUGUST 3RD, 1965)

My grandfather, Rabbi Abraham Cronbach (z"l), was a quiet man, but also a man of depth and spiritual power. Being a Reform Jew, he felt that ritual should be a promise of righteous action, and nothing more. So he lived his ritual in the street. He became the rabbi for Julius and Ethel Rosenberg, accused and murdered by the government for allegedly giving nuclear secrets to the Soviet Union. He even went so far as to meet with President Eisenhower to plead for clemency on their behalf.

He was also the official chaplain for the 'hobos' of America; he reached out to them en-masse and individually. Hobos were a phenomenon of the depression. They rode the rails across this great country—working, begging, and huddling together against the chill of abject poverty. What most people don't know is that they had a loose organization and a unique way of communicating with each other.

Whenever a hobo would arrive in a town, he would go from house to house, like the Hasidic beggars of old; and if he received a hand-out at a particular house, he would put a tiny mark on the door to let his brothers and sisters in poverty know that 'here,' at least, 'one could get a decent meal, a little money or a piece of clothing.' Needless to say, my grandfather was an easy touch and his house was quickly 'marked.' Nevertheless, just after each hobo would leave, my grandmother, who was also a loving soul---but just a bit more practical than my grandfather---would erase the mark put on the door by the recipient of their generosity. But still they kept on coming! So one day after she had erased the mark, she hung around a little while longer only to find my grandfather out on the stoop, putting the mark back up!

Every day I bless my grandfather for *getting out there and teaching.*

RABBI MAURICE DAVIS
(DECEMBER 15ᵀᴴ, 1920 - DECEMBER 14ᵀᴴ, 1993)

It was a couple of days before my *bar mitzvah,* and I was filled with many strong emotions. I was nervous and excited, and also honored. My Torah portion, chosen by my father, Rabbi Maurice Davis *(z"l),* the rabbi of the congregation, was *Kedoshim.* The choice of that portion—for it was not the *sidra* for the *Shabbos* of my *bar mitzvah*—was dripping with meaning. The portion itself is very powerful; but for my father, it was made more powerful by the fact that he had chosen it as the *Sidra d'Kehillah,* the portion of the congregation. As a matter of fact, on the front of the building was a huge black filigree depiction of the *Luḥot ha-Brit* overlaid on a Torah with the words *Kedoshim T'hiyu,* "You Shall be Holy," written in Hebrew across the front. My father had designed it.

The portion also held significant meaning for my grandfather, who had been my father's *rebbe* at Hebrew Union College, the Reform Jewish seminary. My grandfather had been raised in that very congregation, and had read that same Torah portion for his *bar mitzvah* over half a century before. And in a few days, I would stand between these two giants and read that same portion in that same congregation.

One night, before the big day, I came to my father with a thought that had been blossoming in my heart for a while. "Pop," I said to him, "I want to wear a *kippah* for my *bar mitzvah."* This may sound like a strange request, if you are unaware of the politics of the Reform movement in the early 1960s; but it was rare to see a Reform Jew wearing a *kippah* at that time. The

Reform movement had preached that the social and moral laws of Judaism were Eternal, but the ritual laws and customs of our faith were temporal and time-contextual. Neither my father nor my grandfather wore a *kippah*. Both were knowledgeable, involved and religious Jews, but not in the way that an Orthodox Jew would define the term. Both were highly moral men, and that morality was born of Torah study, the prophets and Talmud; but neither man was moved by ritual accoutrement. So here I was, the son and grandson of the Reform rabbis, asking to wear a *kippah* on my *bar mitzvah!*

Well, my father's immediate answer was, "No, that would not be appropriate." I was upset, but did not push the issue. Later that night, my father was sitting on my bed with me and laughed suddenly, saying, "Do you know what is wrong with 'knee-jerk' reactions? When you give a knee-jerk reaction, you are usually being a jerk. I was being a jerk this afternoon," he said. "Of course, if you wish, you may wear a *kippah* on the day of your *bar mitzvah*. But," becoming serious, he said, "we do not do things for show and tell. If you wear one on the day of your *bar mitzvah,* you are making a commitment to wear one whenever you enter a synagogue, and whenever you pray."

Every morning, as I put on my *kippah,* before I don *tallit* and *t'fillin,* I think of the teaching that I received from my father that night. I still have the *kippah* that my father gave me on the day of my *bar mitzvah.*

Every day, I bless my father for *getting out there and teaching.*

RABBI ZALMAN SCHACHTER-SHALOMI
(AUGUST 17TH, 1924 – JULY 3RD, 2014)

A few years after my father passed away, I met the only person who could fill the shoes of Rabbi Abraham Cronbach and Rabbi Maurice Davis, as my *rebbe.* In Reb Zalman, like my father and grandfather, I found a *rebbe* who taught with actions. He reached out to us all with heartfelt support and a supporting heart.

Once, when I was having trouble reaching out to God, when I

was blocked and could not call out in my pain to the Wholly One of Being, Reb Zalman opened the gates for me. I remember sitting in his little *"shtieble"* that day, giving him my *kvittel* (petitionary note), and he responded by asking me about my relationship with my parents. I told him that when I needed the comfort of an ear and a heart, I would turn to my mother, and that when I needed a mindful approach to a problem and the heart-full power of a hug, I went to my father. He then gave me a two-part teaching that I remember in this way:

> We cannot approach God in the realm of *Atzilut*, 'emanation,' for there is no separation there, and therefore no possibility of approach. In the realm of *B'riyah*, 'creation,' we feel the immenseness of the Wholly One of Being, the Source of all Creation. But it is difficult to approach the "non-corporeal" indivisible One except in awe. And in the realm of *Assiyah*, the realm of our weekday, work-a-day lives, our view of reality might become a stumbling block to the closeness that we all need. But, in the emotional world of *Yetzirah*, that formative realm, that place that holds the child in all of us, we can find the approachable God, loving, caring, and in my case, mothering.

In *Yetzirah*, God sits at the kitchen table and listens, cares and loves. And now, when I *davven*, there are wonderful moments in which the gates to heaven open and I find myself sitting at the Holy kitchen table, comforted in the intuitive assurance that God, the mother is listening non-judgmentally, openly, honestly, heartfully, soulfully, and fully. For this, the first part of his teaching I am eternally grateful.

And the second part of the teaching, you might ask? That was a good, long, and powerful hug. It brought back a feeling that I had missed everyday since the day my father had passed away.

And every day, I bless my *rebbe* for *getting out there and teaching.*

Reb Zalman was a man whose *Gevurah* was *Ḥesed*, whose

discipline was compassion. As we read in the *T'fillah—Attah gebore l'olam, Adonai, m'hayay matim attah, rav l'hoshiya,* "You are the *gebor,* the source of *Gevurah,* Oh Wholly One of Being, for you bring life to the dead, you are the fount of all salvation." To me this, the beginning of the second blessing in the *T'fillah,* brings to light the message that God's *Gevurah* is *Hesed.* This is a lesson that I have learned from the Lubavitcher Rebbe and the three rebbes in my life—my father, my grandfather, and my Reb Zalman.

And I thank them all for *getting out there and teaching.*

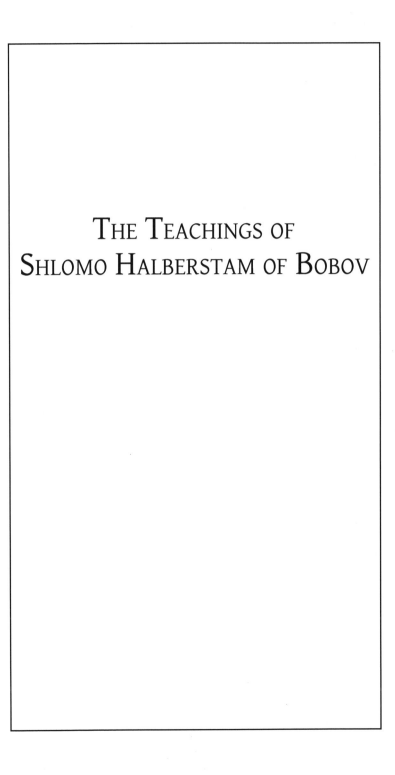

THE TEACHINGS OF
SHLOMO HALBERSTAM OF BOBOV

Trees, Vineyards, and the Master Gardener
Reflections on the Art of Spiritual Guidance

Thomas Atum O'Kane

Editor's Introduction

This reflection on Reb Zalman is inspired by two particular meetings Reb Zalman had with the fourth Bobover Rebbe, Rabbi Shlomo Halberstam, who was from the same region as Reb Zalman's own family. The stories of those two meetings go like this:

At the time of his first meeting with the Bobover Rebbe, Reb Zalman was a Ḥasid of the seventh Lubavitcher Rebbe. Nevertheless, he found that he enjoyed visiting Bobov from time to time. But soon he began to feel like "a man with a wife and a mistress," so he came to the Bobover Rebbe and said: "I already have a Rebbe. I'm a Lubavitcher Ḥasid; but I come here to share the warmth."

To this, the Bobover Rebbe replied, "And you are welcome here. But, you know, one may have an apple tree that bears Golden Delicious apples, and if one grafts a sprig from a Macintosh apple tree to it, in time it will grow to be part of that tree and bear fruit also. From the Macintosh branch will come Golden Delicious apples, and from the main tree branches will come Macintosh apples."

On another occasion, Reb Zalman sought the Bobover Rebbe's counsel at a time when he felt he was burning-out. With the demands of his teaching career, lecturing around the country, and guiding individuals, it seemed to him that the deep contemplative practices he had done to cultivate his soul were being neglected. So he asked, "What can I do for these people if I cannot do the same for myself anymore?" The Bobover Rebbe replied, " 'They have asked you to tend their vineyard, but your own vineyard you have not kept.' Nevertheless, because you have tended their vineyard dutifully, the Shekhinah, the Divine Presence will give you a double portion for your own."

Here, Thomas Atum O'Kane, a Sufi teacher and close personal student of both Reb Zalman and Pir Vilayat Inayat-Khan, remembers Reb Zalman as the Master Gardener.

— N.M-Y., editor

KNOWING THE NAME

WHEN I FIRST MET REB ZALMAN, I felt both overwhelmed and scared to death. He wasn't anything like the religious figures of my childhood—Roman Catholic priests and nuns. He was juicy with life and a huge overflowing heart. Nor was he like my Sufi master, Pir Vilayat Inayat-Khan, with whom I was studying. Reb Zalman was sensual, his God delicious, and he had embraced the full spectrum of life's experiences. I left our initial encounter in a state of bewilderment. That night, I saw Reb Zalman in a dream saying to me, "I have come to help you become who you really are." There was no way for me to ignore such direct guidance, so I made another appointment with him; but this time, even more afraid than before.

When I told him about the dream, he said, "You already have a teacher; so just think of me as your Jewish spiritual uncle. There are questions and issues that you can bring to your uncles that you wouldn't take to your father." Later, I realized just how much his response was really a marriage of wisdom and compassion. He wanted to honor both my relationship with Pir Vilayat and the guidance of the dream. He provided me with a name and a container for the guidance to unfold. The idea of the "spiritual uncle" was perfect; because the personal problems I took to him, and issues related to our often not-so-noble human journey were not the domain of Pir Vilayat. These two men have been the central pillars of my spiritual life, and its poles also; but because Reb Zalman had the capacity to name an inclusive form, I never felt the slightest conflict within my heart between my two teachers. He knew that one teacher may not hold all the qualities your soul needs for its unfoldment; and, in this world of forms, it is important to name the essential relationships.

VINEYARDS AND THE MASTER GARDENER

About ten years ago, I went to lunch with Reb Zalman at a market where he lives in Boulder, and our time there was marked by a continuous flow of people stopping to greet him. I studied the effect of each exchange. Each person responded like a flower that had just been watered after a hot and dry day. Clearly, each person had felt met, seen, connected with and opened. There were no long conversations about spiritual matters, nor was Reb Zalman invoking the role of 'the teacher.' He was simply doing what had become completely natural to him, tending a garden of souls. The garden extended to all he encountered, and from years of gardening, he knew just the right kind of soil, the right mixture of sun and shade, the proper amount of water, when to prune, and what went together as he cared for each flower or plant.

It is a temptation for those in the helping professions to identify with the beauty that unfolds in those you work with while not tending to the divine seeds in your own soul-plot. For over four decades, Reb Zalman has mentored me in the art of spiritual guidance, and I would like to offer here some the most useful teachings I have learned from this Master Gardener on the subject. For the most part, they concern caring for your own soul while still answering the call of spiritual service, and give us insight into how Reb Zalman found his own balance, and in how the Rebbe's blessing flowered into wisdom.

Gardening Tips

One day, it occurred to me that if I answered this 'call,' I would spend the rest of my life listening to the difficulties and sufferings of the human journey. It felt like a crushing weight that would certainly bury my future. I was then in my middle thirties and Reb Zalman gave me this very sage advice, "In a few years, you will have heard all the basic patterns underlying human problems. What keeps it alive, and your heart engaged, is the uniqueness of each person and the particular details."

He directed my attention to the unique expression of the desire in each person and their story, rather than only recognizing the archetypes. It has been said that God's favorite thing is stories, which is why God created people. Sometimes I feel God has shared with me His/Her favorite practice, listening to the stories of individuals. Rather than the burden my soul feared, Reb Zalman showed me a way to enrich my soul with stories.

* * *

He once said to me, "Your generation knows when to put the robe on, and when to take it off. The past generation always wore the robe." He was conveying the importance of knowing when to wear the robe of spiritual guide and teacher, and when to let go of the robe and claim your own personal life and journey. The danger of always being clothed in the robe is the loss of one's own personal relationship with the divine, which is precious and particular.

Once, Reb Zalman asked me to accompany him to a wedding he was performing. This involved several hours in the car going and returning. Somewhere along the way, he said, "I asked you to come, because with you, I don't have to always be 'on,'—placed continuously in the role of teacher." This comment re-affirmed for me the value of resting in oneself and one's own life, rather than always relating through the role. It taught me to seek out relationships where I do not always have to wear the "robe."

* * *

The value of dialogue with God is central to the Jewish tradition, and this is an area that Reb Zalman has made tangible for me. He taught me that if you are doing God's work, you have the right to ask for what you need. Coming from a Roman Catholic background, there were certain things that were not topics of polite conversation with God. Learning to recognize needs, and then to ask regarding them were significant practices that have fed and continue to feed my soul, and give it a voice. If you are going to work together, there has to be a voice for exchange.

* * *

Burn-out comes when you have lost your own center, becoming possessed by the archetype of the helper. I once went to Reb Zalman in this condition. He suggested that I do a short retreat on the theme of dying. He said, while lying down, I should let go of each of the responsibilities that were defining me, until the soul could remember its natural condition of spacious freedom. I had gotten lost in the divine exhalation of unfoldment through life, and he reminded me of the soul's need for inhalation, turning within, returning home, absorbed in the Source.

* * *

As he aged, Reb Zalman became more discerning about how he invested his energy. He told me some years ago, "I used to make my future schedule when I was on a high after some good program. I felt unlimited in my capacity at that time; but later, my poor body would have to live out the unrealistic commitments I had made. Now, I schedule when I am tired." This leaves some openings so the soul can be fed, and the body cared for.

* * *

Once, Reb Zalman asked me if I would go with him to a program "with the group that is the most difficult for me." He did a great job and everyone left inspired. Afterwards, he had arranged for a small room to which he invited a few people for prayer, practice and singing. It was so beautiful and intimate. In doing this, he gave his soul and ours the accommodation space for "a double portion of the Divine Presence."

* * *

In the last several years, I have witnessed Reb Zalman in the midst of a struggle and a dance between two dimensions of the divine: the full embrace of the wonder of life through appreciation and compassion; and the longing for space and solitude (he once said to me that "God shares His/Her loneliness with the atheist"). In some ways, the hermit in him was the more un-lived life that comes knocking at the door, asking to be met. Many years ago, he taught me how to give the hermit a space in the life of service. He said, "No matter what you are doing, or who you are with, you can always ask for a few moments of silence. It may be a brief meeting, yet it will offer a great depth and renewal."

* * *

Over forty years have passed since I had that remarkable dream of Reb Zalman. He has been the Master Gardener who has tended the divine seeds in me, and who has helped me to realize possibilities that I could sense, but not really imagine. I am one in a vast and amazing garden of souls that he has tended. How blessed we all are.

How Will God
Bring Us Back to Zion?
Ḥoni ha-Magel, Ecology, and the Paradigm Shift

Maggid Michael L. Kagan

The following teaching is inspired by a mashal or 'parable' of the fourth Bobover Rebbe, Rabbi Shlomo Halberstam, as heard by Reb Zalman sometime in the 1960s. Here, Maggid Michael Kagan, an Israeli scientist and teacher of Holistic Judaism, gives a Talmudic reflection on it, drawing on the well-known story to Ḥoni ha-Magel.

— N.M-Y., editor.

REB ZALMAN HEARD THIS teaching directly from the fourth Bobover Rebbe, Rabbi Shlomo Halberstam in New York:

> A *tzaddik* is said to be "good" and to receive the reward for the good that is done, and the reward for the fruit of these actions as well. That is to say, a *tzaddik* gets the capital, the interest, and the compound interest. However, one who does evil receives punishment only for the evil, and not for the fruit of their actions as well.
>
> Why should this be?
>
> If a *tzaddik* gives a dollar to someone in need, it is not just the exchange of a dollar from one person to another, but that dollar is also intended for help and for benefit: to get

food, to meet the needs of a family, and for various other good things. However, the thief who steals a dollar usually means to steal a dollar to gratify only his own needs. So the one who gives good receives the reward also for the many good intentions; while the one who intends evil is punished only for that evil.[1]

Somehow this wonderful teaching reminds me of the story of Ḥoni ha-Magel (Ḥoni the Circle-Drawer) found in the Talmud:

R. Yoḥanan bar Nafḥa said: This righteous man [Ḥoni] was throughout the whole of his life troubled about the meaning of the verse: *A Song of Ascents, When the Lord brought back the returnees to Zion, we were like dreamers.* 'Is it possible for a man to dream continuously for seventy years?' One day he was journeying on the road and he saw a man planting a carob tree; he asked him: "How long does it take [for this tree] to bear fruit?" The man replied: "Seventy years." He then asked him: "Are you certain that you will live another seventy years?" The man replied: "I found [ready grown] carob trees in the world; as my forefathers planted these for me, so I too plant these for my children."

Ḥoni sat down to have a meal and sleep overcame him. As he slept, a rocky formation enclosed upon him which hid him from sight and he continued to sleep for seventy years. When he awoke, he saw a man gathering the fruit of the carob tree and he asked him: "Are you the man who planted the tree?" The man replied: "I am his grandson." Thereupon he exclaimed: "It is clear then that I have slept for seventy years." He then caught sight of his donkey that had meanwhile given birth to several generations. And he returned to his house. There he enquired: "Is the son of

1 A *mashal* of the fourth Bobover Rebbe, Rabbi Shlomo Halberstam, heard by Rabbi Zalman Schachter-Shalomi in the 1960s. On Monday, August 12th, 2002, Reb Zalman told the *mashal* to the editor of this volume, Netanel Miles-Yépez, while on the way back from Ruach HaAretz at Shambhala Mountain Center in Red Feather Lakes, Colorado, and asked him to memorize it for future Ḥasidim.

Honi ha-Magel still alive?" The people answered him: "His son is no more, but his grandson is still living." Thereupon he said to them: "I am Honi ha-Magel," but no one would believe him. He then went to the *Beit ha-Midrash* and there he overheard the scholars say: "The law is as clear to us as in the days of Honi ha-Magel; for whenever he came to the *Beit ha-Midrash* he would settle for the scholars any difficulty that they had." Whereupon he called out: "I am he!" but the scholars would not believe him, nor did they give him his due honor. This hurt him greatly and he prayed [for death] and he died.[1]

What a strange story. Let's take it apart.

Honi appears to have been a scholar-shaman who lived in the century before the destruction of the Temple. He is only mentioned twice in the whole Talmud, in this section and the proceeding one, in which he prays for rain using his famous circle-drawing trick. In this story, Honi is described as a *tzaddik,* a righteous person. Is this honorific endowed upon him because he is a shaman, a scholar, or because of his piety and good deeds? The story will tell. The verse that troubled him in the story is from Psalm 126, which we are familiar with from the Blessing After Meals. The psalm consists of six versus, all of which have something to tell us about Honi.

The first is about dreams and dreamers. Honi asks: *What does it mean that upon their return, the exiles where like dreamers?* Honi takes this absolutely literally, which would mean that since the Babylonian exile was for seventy years, the exiles must have been asleep, dreaming for seventy years. *That's not possible,* says Honi, which is a strange thing for a miracle-maker to say. Does he deny the possibility that God can do anything? If he can draw a simple circle in the dust and cry out to the Creator of heaven and earth to make it rain, being able turn 'the faucet' on and off at will, then what's his problem? Perhaps he suffers from the bane of

---

1 Talmud, Ta'anit 23b. By coincidence, this was, the *daf yomi* on the day that Reb Zalman died.

every magician, the longing for the ultimate trick—the Prestige?

Or perhaps the story is a subtle attack against all of us so-called 'sophisticated students' of sacred texts who see metaphors and similes and worlds upon worlds behind every letter and word, and even the spaces between them. Because obviously it says *keholmim*—'like dreamers'—so of course it is a simile; they weren't *actually* asleep, dreaming! The psalmist is surely saying that the return to the Land after 70 years of exile was like a dream come true.

Or is it in the sense of . . . *What? Back already? Pinch me—I must be dreaming!*

Or perhaps dreaming is not to be taken as synonymous with sleeping, but rather with hoping *(tikva)*. So it would read: *How is it possible to hold on to the hope for redemption for so long?* Or in the mouth of a Zionist: *Is it really possible to hold on to the dream of returning to our land for two thousand years?*

Or, like the Berditchever Rebbe, perhaps Ḥoni is asking God why it took seventy years to end the exile? *If God can bring rain in minutes, why not bring the redemption* (Mashiaḥ) *now?*

Or is exile an existential state of non-reality like sleeping. Redemption is the state of being truly awake, just as portrayed in *The Matrix*. So Ḥoni's question becomes: *Is it really possible for people to be asleep (ignorant) for so long? In fact, for their entire lives?*

However, Ḥoni is not 'sophisticated' like us. He sees the world differently. Perhaps he sees the world as it truly is; for Ḥoni—to use one of Reb Zalman's favorite expressions—is a *Pashute Yid*, 'a simple Jew,' a Jew in child's mind (as opposed to 'monkey mind'), an aboriginal Jew, a Jew from Chelm, a Jew who loves *p'shat*. In fact, the use of the word 'child' and 'innocence' are leitmotifs that run consistently through both stories. And, as we all know, the gift of prophecy exists today only in the mouths of children and fools.[1] His relationship to God is like that of a child to his father, he will demand and cry until he gets what he wants. And if it's not enough, then he will cry some more.

---

1 Talmud, Baba Batra 12b.

But Ḥoni is not a child. His motivations are not for self-fulfillment or self-aggrandizement, but as it says in the 3rd verse of the psalm: "The LORD has done great things to us; we rejoiced." It is all for the aggrandizement of God; it's all for the power of wow!

Simple . . . but not so simple; for our story suggests that Ḥoni was not only innocent like a child, but also childish. What better characterizes a childish mind than the need for instant gratification? "I want it, and I want it now!" The future doesn't matter; in fact, it doesn't exist. There's only now! Ḥoni sees a man planting a carob tree and asks him why he bothers, since he will never live long enough to benefit from its offspring? The man answers by saying that, as his ancestors planted trees that he now benefits from, so he will plant trees for his offspring to benefit from. The question that Ḥoni asks is a childish question. It comes from a place desirous of instant satisfaction where, like the rain, you ask and you get. Everyone in their right mind (or is it, left brain?) knows that if you don't plant today there will be nothing for tomorrow. This, of course, reminds us of the saying of the Bobover Rebbe, that altruistic actions have a ripple effect, and the *tzaddik* receives the rewards for all the offspring, and the offspring's offspring when his intention is for the greater good, and not just for the value of the limited act of kindness.

So at this point the question must be asked: In the story so far, who is the *tzaddik?* Ḥoni or the carob-tree planter? It seems that the latter more closely fits the description through his altruistic act of loving-kindness. Or maybe Ḥoni is indeed a *tzaddik,* just one living on a different plane of existence than we do, in which there are no worries about the future, since God is here, now and immediate.

So Ḥoni sits down to have a meal, and maybe like Rip van Winkle, he drinks too much and falls asleep. He sleeps and sleeps for seventy years. But this is not a Rip van Winkle story (who slept for only twenty winks (years); for does it not say that the earth wrapped itself around him and hid him safe within her womb? The Divine Mother, it seems, is looking-out for her child. When he awakes, he sees on the spot where the man had been planting seeds or a seedling, a fully mature carob tree filled with ripe carob pods. And there is also a man who resembles the planter, now picking the fruit. But it is not the man; it is his grandson! Honi discovers—presumably to his shock and disbelief—that he has slept for seventy years. So it can be done, with God's help. Now he knows. End of a life-time of enquiry. End of story.

Really?

So why a carob tree? In fact, why a tree at all? Within the story, the carob tree acts as a trigger point because it is assumed that it takes seventy years from planting to maturation. Seventy years to bear fruit against seventy years of exile. But, apparently, carob pods will appear within the relatively short time of 3-4 years if the starting point is a cutting, 6-8 years from seedling, and up to 15 years from seeds.

> Description: The carob tree is a slow growing, medium sized evergreen tree originating in the eastern Mediterranean. It is a member of the Legume (Pea) family and is the only member of the genus Ceratonia. It is a xerophilous scleophphyllous species well suited to dry infertile environments. The species is trioecious with male, female and hermaphrodite inflorescences and is often multi stemmed growing up to 15 meters in height. The production of fruit begins around the age of 15 and continues for the life of the plant. The leaves are broad, dark green and offering substantial shade. The pods are long and leathery often growing up to 300mm long.
>
> The seeds from the Carob tree are extremely consistent in size and weight and are believed to have been the original gauge for the 'carat' used by jewelers.[1]

So maybe the man who planted the tree was simply wrong. Or perhaps the carob is being used for other purposes other than the fact that it takes 15 long years to yield fruit, perhaps, dare I

---

1 Http://www.carobana.com.au/carob.html, accessed on July 10th, 2014.

say it, metaphorically? And now I'm going out on a bit of a limb. The Hebrew for carob is *ḥaruv*. This is the same root as *ḥorev*—the "Mountain of the Lord," where Torah was given. The meaning of both is *ḥareva,* meaning 'dryness' (as in Exodus 14:21). And, as it says above, the tree survives in dry, hostile climates where its fruit can be life-preserving. (There is also the legend that Rabbi Shimon bar Yohai survived 12 years in a cave just on carob fruit from a tree that miraculously appeared already bearing fruit.[1] In fact, he liked it so much that he went back for another year.) So perhaps the carob is symbolic for the Torah that was given in such a dry place, but which is as living water for the spirit, as alluded to in the 4th verse of the Psalm: *"Turn our captivity, O LORD, as the streams in the dry land."*

Or, alternatively, the story may be emphasizing the durability of the exiles in a place of spiritual barrenness?

Or maybe it is the fact that carob pods make a tasty and healthy chocolate-spread loved by children?

And a tree? Because the human being is likened to a tree, as it says: "A person is like the tree of a field" (Deut. 20:19), and therefore, our children are like the fruit of the tree. And you should know that one of Reb Zalman's favorite blessings is that which is said over the blossoming fruit trees exclusively in the month of Nisan. Why only in Nisan? Because that is the month when we relate to our children (our fruit) about what it is to be free and all the myriad things there are to be thankful for.[2]

After Ḥoni's self-revelation that he is still alive in this world, he runs home, only to find that the fruit of his loins has passed on. His grandson, Abba Ḥilkiyah, however, is still alive and well.[3] He makes a vain attempt to persuade everyone that he is Ḥoni back from the dead. He wishes, in fact, to fulfill the 6th verse of the Psalm: *"Though he who goes on his way weeping bearing the measure of seed, he shall come home with joy, bearing his sheaves."* Which reminds me of the movie, The Return of Martin Guerre, in which

---

1 Talmud, Shabbat 33b.

2 Michael L. Kagan, *The Holistic Haggadah* (Urim, 2004), 31.

3 The next story is about him and his wife's abilities also to bring rain.

a villager in 16ᵗʰ-century France, goes off to war, disappears, and is presumed dead. (The word *guerre* means 'war' in French, and its trans-linguistic pun means 'stranger' in Hebrew.) A number of years later, he or someone very much like him, returns. Could it really be him? Some believe him, while some don't. For Ḥoni, the matter is far more delicate—he has been away for two generations! There's no one left alive who could have known him except perhaps for the children who are now old. Why would anyone believe him?

He runs desperately to the *beit midrash* where they are still quoting his pearls of wisdom. But there too, no one believes that he is he. And since he is not given his due honor, he prays to die and, of course, since it's Ḥoni, the Holy Father listens, obeys, and Ḥoni dies.

What does the text mean by, "not giving him his due honor"? And why did it hurt him so? Why couldn't he live up to the 5ᵗʰ verse of the psalm? *"They that sow in tears shall reap in joy."* Since when does a *tzaddik* seek honor above his own life? Within the context of the story, as I have presented it, this attitude is consistent with the side of Ḥoni's personality that is more childish, almost autistic, in behavior. It is the need of a child to be seen, to be noticed, to be acknowledged: "Daddy! Mummy! Look at me!" Without this, it is as if he doesn't existence; and when Ḥoni doesn't get this recognition, he desires to leave this plane of existence.

But I want to zoom out and look at the story from the broader perspective of the whole *sugiya,* or section of the Talmud. I am of the school of thought that every story and every quote is brought in order to shine light on an overarching discussion, and not just by association. The entire tractate of Ta'anit, which is the central tractate of the entire Talmud, deals with the question of the power of prayer in our relationship with God, especially after the destruction of the Temple and the start of the 2000-year exile.[1]

---

1 Thus it has been taught to me by my *ḥevruta*, Rabbi Yedidya Sinclair. I also want to thank my son Itai Kagan for his help in analyzing the variations of this story that exist in Mishnah, the Tosefta and the Yerushalmi Talmud.

As Rabbi Eleazer ben Perata said: "Ever since the destruction of the Temple the rain has come with difficulty." God manifests God's-self through rain since, in Israel, rain is life. When we are in exile, God is in exile, and the rain is no longer regular, and life is more difficult. This *sugiya* tackles the transition between the two states.

So what's happening here on the macro level? I conjecture that the story of Ḥoni is being brought as part of the bigger debate that starts at the beginning of this tractate and carries on throughout, namely the debate between Rabbi Eliezer and Rabbi Yehoshua about the meaning of prayer, nature, and our relationship with God. Part of this debate appears in the famous story of the Akhnai oven.[1] Rabbi Eliezer calls upon miracle after miracle (note that the first two involve a carob tree and water) to support his side in the halachic argument, eventually bringing the Divine voice to confirm his position. Each move is parried by Rabbi Yehoshua, until finally Rabbi Yehoshua declares: "Not in Heaven!" meaning, *halakhah* is to be determined by human intellect alone, without the intervention of anything beyond, even God. (To which God is said to have chuckled, saying: "My children have defeated Me.") Result: Rabbi Eliezer is excommunicated.

Clearly Ḥoni is a miracle-maker, and I am assuming that Rabbi Eliezer feels a certain amount of identification and empathy for him. However, I sense that the Talmudic editor is bringing the second story of Ḥoni, namely the piece quoted in the name of R. Yohanan, to disparage and discredit Ḥoni, and by implication, Rabbi Eliezer. I can almost hear a sarcastic tone in R. Yohanan's voice when he introduces Ḥoni as the *"tzaddik."* It is as if he is saying, "Yeah, right, some *tzaddik;* all the time he was only after his own aggrandizement." The age of miracle-makers is dead; long live the head.

Nevertheless, the story of Ḥoni has important lessons, in spite of Ḥoni. The obvious one is that of inter-generational responsibility, especially with regard to ecology and environmental concerns. We must take care today for tomorrow's tomorrow, even if

---

1 Talmud, Baba Metzia 59b.

we will not see that tomorrow ourselves. Short-term, selfish planning will deprive our grandchildren of the magnificent and beautiful world that we have been privileged to live in. In this sense, perhaps, as I suggested earlier, in the eyes of the Bobover's lesson, the planter of the carob tree is the *tzaddik*. And Ḥoni? Perhaps he is the thief depriving his grandchildren the fruits that he himself enjoyed. Is that not a form of thievery? Isn't that what we are doing by depleting the world of its energy sources, of polluting the air and waters, over-fishing, over-fertilizing, over-mining, over-feeding?

But enough of this preaching.

Another aspect of the Ḥoni story is that of paradigm shift. (Now you know for sure that this was written in honor of Reb Zalman.) Ḥoni sleeps for 70 years, and when he awakes, he is in a different world, a world that he hardly recognizes, a world that certainly doesn't recognize him. He is only remembered by some of the things he said on those occasions that he went to the *beit midrash.* Think of where you are today; think about where you came from; think about what you were like before you became who you are now. Obviously time has passed, maybe even 70 years; but it is not a matter of aging. It is a matter of being. I am hardly recognizable to my past. Think of Reb Zalman as a young Lubavitcher, and then think of what he became . . . Paradigm shifts.

Another paradigm shift is highlighted in the ongoing disagreements between Rabbi Eliezer and Rabbi Yehoshua, which, as I have already mentioned, run throughout this tractate. They had very different approaches to the traumatic changes that took place in their lifetimes, namely the end of the Temple epoch and the beginning of the second exile. Rabbi Eliezer was known for his conservatism ("Like a cistern that never loses a drop"), which is one approach to the times that are a-changing. Rabbi Yehoshua was far more daring in his recognition that the old model needs to be buried and the new model turned on. It was for this that Rabbi Eliezer was ex-communicated. But when it came time for Rabbi Eliezer to die, Rabbi Yehoshua came to his bedside and declared: "O master, you are of more value to Israel than God's gift of the rain; since the rain gives life in this world only, whereas you give life both in this world and in the world to come."[1] Note once again the references to rain.

We are now living in the throes of a new paradigm shift. We have returned to our Land and the exile is ending. Jews and Judaism are struggling to redefine themselves. It is not an easy process; we do not know how long this transition will take; we cannot know what the world will look like on the other side. We can only pray that whatever we are doing now will help effect a safe and rapid shift to the next level of human consciousness, in which our children's children will enjoy the wow of now and offer thanksgiving to God for having had such wise ancestors.

Finally, I would like to bring Reb Zalman's wonderful translation of Psalm 126.

PSALM 126
A Reaching Up Song

We dream
How God will bring us back to Zion.
Then shall we laugh again.
Then shall we sing again.
Then people will say:
"How great it is!
Look what *Yah* has done for them!
If only *Yah* had done the same for us,
We too would now be glad."

Oh God! Why don't You bring us back?
As you bring back water

---

1 Mek., Yitro, 10.

To the dried-up Negev gulches.

Yes we will trust. We sowed with tears
We will reap with song.

Those who go, casting out seeds,
Sometimes feel like weeping.
Yet they go on, always trusting,
That they shall come back singing.
Bearing in the harvest sheaves.

THE HEALING QUESTION
Transforming the World with Non-violence

RABBI LYNN GOTTLIEB

The following teaching is inspired by a mashal *or 'parable' of the fourth Bobover Rebbe, Rabbi Shlomo Halberstam, as heard by Reb Zalman sometime in the 1960s. Here, Rabbi Lynn Gottlieb, Reb Zalman's first woman ordinee and a spiritual activist, retells it and gives a modern* perush, *or interpretation of it.*

— N.M-Y., editor

REB ZALMAN ONCE HEARD the following mashal, or teaching-story from the Bobover Rebbe in New York:

Once there was a kingdom where the first still was invented. Before long, everyone had their own still and was making their own schnapps. And drinking it, too! That year, the farmers of that kingdom neither planted nor plowed, nor did much of anything else, because they were too busy drinking schnapps. All the time. As a result, the kingdom suffered from a shortage of food.

The king's chief advisor went to the king and reported the situation. "There is no harvest in your kingdom this year because all the farmers are drunk on schnapps." The king issued a decree to solve the problem: " 'Anyone caught drinking schnapps will be punished!' That should stop them from drinking!" declared the king. But the very next harvest season, there was nothing to harvest because all the farmers were drunk on schnapps. So the king decided to personally investigate the problem. He left the palace and walked with his retinue through the countryside until he came to a farmhouse. He knocked on the door, but no one answered. He knocked harder and announced himself. Still, no answer. The king opened the door of the farmhouse and entered. The place was a mess. He looked around and spied a pair of legs sticking out from under a table. The king crouched down and saw a drunk farmer sipping on a bottle of schnapps, too afraid to defy the king openly, but not afraid enough to stop drinking under the table.

"You know, farmer, I must punish you now!" warned the king. "I know, your highness," says the farmer and wipes his mouth with his sleeve. "However," says the king, "I can't give you the appropriate punishment until I understand the nature of your crime. Do you have some of the schnapps left?"

"Here, your highness!" The farmer gives the king the little bit of schnapps he has left in the bottle. The king takes a swig and immediately spits it out. *"Fehhh! . . . I can't punish you further for drinking this! This is punishment enough!"*

So it is with *Ribbono Shel Olam* who has given us a Guide by which to live. When we sin against it, He comes to dole out our just punishment, but figures to do it right, He must 'taste' a bit of our sin. And when He does so, He spits it out immediately and can't bring Himself to punish us more, for the sin is its own punishment.[1]

---

1 A *mashal* of the fourth Bobover Rebbe, Rabbi Shlomo Halberstam, heard by Rabbi Zalman Schachter-Shalomi in the 1960s. On Monday, August 12th, 2002, Reb Zalman told the *mashal* to the editor of this volume while on the way back from Ruach HaAretz at Shambhala Mountain Center in Red Feather Lakes, Colorado, and asked him to memorize it for future Ḥasidim.

What is the healing question inside the story, since all teaching stories in Judaism are grounded in this concern? Healing is the way of the heart that restores our spiritual wholeness, renews our relationships and overcomes brokenness. But what is the nature of healing? How does it work?

We have learned from history, and trial and error, that harsh punishments, threats, and acts of revenge do not lead to healing and reconciliation. Rather, these types of reaction to *'het'* and violence harden hearts, entrench fear, and increase isolation in the human experience.

As a result of violence, one can get used to bitterness and self-loathing. Such feelings can fill us with despair and cause us to believe we are unworthy of blessings or unable to change. We may isolate ourselves, 'get high' under a table and abandon hope for peace and well-being. To hide our true condition, we may put on a mask of acceptability when we move in the world. Nonetheless, our legs are sticking out from under the table in full view of all those who take the time to look.

Perhaps our condition fills us with rage, and we blame others because we see ourselves as victims. We become imprisoned by our sense of outrage at those who hurt us and cut ourselves off from the possibility of reconciliation. Perhaps we feel entitled to our way of life and see those who suffer as somehow deserving of their suffering. This frame of mind causes us to rationalize our reliance upon afflictive emotions to interpret and shape the conflicts in our daily lives. We flounder in the face of our own frailness and forget how to tap into our beauty, our capacity for compassion and our human ability to turn ourselves around.

'Het' also occurs when we forget the web of connection of which we are a part. Unreflective privilege based on gender, race, age, geography, or economic status may cause us to be separated from those who do not enjoy such privilege. Privilege blinds us to the nature of our connections. In assuming privileges of rank rooted in hierarchical systems such as sexism, racism, class and nationality, we impact the health of the entire system. Systemic suffering by some sectors of society is a sign of injustice in

the whole system. When we categorize ourselves in ways that exclude others from the circle of blessings, we divide humanity into 'us and them.'

The human family has wept enough tears to fill an ocean. During the past century, hundreds of millions have perished in the deadly jaws of human violence. How shall we transform the part of our selves and our community which lies drunk with fear and violence underneath the table? What is the nature of the remembrance that will stir our souls to embrace the whole with love, to overcome victimhood and become agents and pursuers of peace?

What is the source of healing that can transform our hearts and cause us to set aside our addictions to violence and denial?

The way of Jewish non-violence, known as *shmirat shalom,* is the best medicine for transforming perpetual states of violence into cultures of *convivencia:* diverse communities that live well together. *Shmirat Shalom* embraces the whole circle of life with the active force of non-violence. Non-violence is a pro-active choice and bestows the blessing of peaceful agency upon its practitioners.

This reminds me of a story: A Jewish sage walked down the street. Two thugs accost her and block her path. One of them shakes his fist in her face. "Hey rabbi, can you guess what's in my hand?" She notices a tiny feather sticking out of his balled up fist. "You're holding a bird."

"That's right, rabbi, it's a bird. But tell me, is the bird alive or dead?"

The rabbi breaths deeply and looks into the eyes of the person standing before her. "I don't know if the bird is alive or dead', says the sage, "but the bird is in your hand."

To move from victimhood to agency, we must realize that the bird is in our hand and we have the power to choose life or death for it. Let us consider faithfulness to a healing path, a path of *shmirat shalom,* a path of non-violence instead of putting our faith in militarism, the force of punishment or separations that harm us rather than heal us. The reward and punishment paradigm never worked. It only perpetuated harm and fear, two ingredients that give rise to violence. Rather, let us extend the awareness of inter-dependence and welcome, loving our neighbor and ourselves, pursuing peace with non-violence as a way to heal our community and the world.

It is possible to overcome our addiction to violence if we commit to Jewish non-violence. To do so, we need both a community and a daily practice. I believe part of the practice should include multi-faith, multi-cultural and inter-generational events on a regular basis that give active, public witness to non-violence as a way of life. Here is one example. There are ten thousand more. The Muslim-Jewish Peacewalk for Interfaith Solidarity was co-created by Abdul Rauf Campos Marquetti and I in Albuquerque, New Mexico, in response to Islamophobia generated by 911. The peacewalk spread to 18 cities throughout the United States and Canada, including Philadelphia, Tucson, and Brooklyn, New York. My congregation, Nahalat Shalom, wanted to respond publicly in protest when Operation Defensive Shield was unleashed in March of 2002, further contributing to the cycle of violence in the Holy Land. We conceived of a pilgrimage. We would walk 6.6 miles on foot to the Islamic Center of New Mexico with the message: "Peace between people is possible." Five days later, 350 caring individuals from a broad spectrum of faith-rooted communities joined Nahalat Shalom and members of the Islamic Center in Albuquerque, New Mexico, for a pilgrimage of hope and reconciliation, and to state clearly that we reject militarism as a faith-rooted response to violence. We were pleased that so many people wanted to express their goodwill toward each other and the Muslim community. Members of the Native American, Buddhist, Chicano, Catholic and Protestant, Sikh, Bahai, Hindu, Muslim and Jewish communities, walked and prayed for peace. Since those days, our witness is still needed, as is our activism in opposition to the corporate and governmental systems that propagate militarism, mass incarceration, and other violations of human rights as defined by the Universal Declaration of Human Rights.

The harvest of non-violence as a Jewish and communal way of life is the creation of 'the beloved community' that has the power to heal the wounds of the past and set forth a new way of being together. The children of the Peacewalk know each other now. They play together, study together, sing and dance together, and share the stories of their lives. As part of a wilderness peace camp that grew out of the peacewalk, children from Jewish, Christian and Muslim communities sat in a healing circle and shared with each other how prejudice impacts their lives. A boy from Yemen, Adnan, related his sorrow and shock when his best friend's parents forbid him from playing at his best friend's house after September 11th. Luckily, Adnan's best friend ignored his parent's bigoted rule and continued his relationship with Adnan. Adnan's sister was not so lucky. Her friends abandoned her, and she sat alone. Adnan began to weep; his small frame shook with sobs. The children sitting nearby reached out and touched him. Many of them cried along with him. The young are wise. They understand the hurtful nature of separation that artificially divides people. At the end of the allotted time in the circle, the children offered each other blessings: a world free of prejudice, violence and fear; a world encircled with a garland of love; a world that finally turns away from the stick and sword, a world where everyone can be friends. Then they went out to play a non-competitive peace game that requires cooperation to complete in a beautiful meadow where sagebrush and pine scent the land with the sweetness of desert, and the sky fills with thunder and rain in the summer afternoon. For the sake of these children, and the children of the human family, we need to reject revenge, militarism and violence, and embrace active non-violence as a Jewish way of life. Let us be impeccable in our teachings, so that we do not add to the atmosphere of hatred or mistrust; but always look for ways to uplift and illuminate the peace that may exist, even if it is only a small and fragile spark. Let us renew our faith the power of non-violence to transform the world.

Dear Zalman, my beloved teacher —

You will always be in my heart as I move through this mysterious and wonderful world. Thank you for opening the way to a new Judaism that rejects triumphalism and embraces the whole world. Thank you for sharing your wisdom and caring with so many thousands of souls, and for bringing so many of our brothers and sisters home. May the light of your blessings continue to illuminate our way. We miss you and love you. Lynn.

THE TEACHINGS OF
GEDALIAH KENIG OF S'FAT

You Have the Da'at You Need

The Way to Become a Kishkes-Jew

Shalvi Schachter Waldman

Editor's Introduction

The following teaching on da'at *by Shalvi Schachter Waldman, a Bratzlaver Ḥasid in S'fat, was inspired by a story her father, Reb Zalman, used to tell about his dear friend, Reb Gedaliah Aharon Kenig, the beloved leader and builder of the Bratzlav community in S'fat, now led by his son, Rabbi Elazar Mordecai Kenig. The story, as Reb Zalman told it, goes like this:*

One day, many years ago, Reb Gedaliah Kenig told me about a man the Jerusalem community intended to censure. A meeting was held in Meah Shearim and people began to get up and accuse and berate this man who somehow wasn't living up to their expectations. So Reb Gedaliah rises and takes out a volume of Rebbe Nahman's *Likkutei MaHaRan*. He ascends the *bima* and says, "I want to read you a teaching of Rebbe Nahman. It begins like this: Be very careful with what you say, because after you have lived your life in this world, you have to pay for the guilt *with-your-mind-on-it* or *with-your-mind-not-on-it*. Furthermore, don't judge anyone too harshly. For when you come to the next world, they will ask you this question, *What do you think should be done*

— 153 —

if somebody has committed such and such a sin? Often, when people are talking to the authorities up in Heaven, they get very pious and say things like, *For such and such a sin— terrible, terrible—five years of shooting, six years of hanging!* But we are taught, 'Before whom will you have to give a law and an account?' Why do you have to tell them in Heaven what the law is? Because when you give the harshest interpretation of that law, they hold you accountable according to that interpretation and say, *Okay, let's see how many times you transgressed it.* Why do they do this? Because your transgression was obviously done *mida'ato,* with your knowledge, by your consent; it was done consciously." Then Reb Gedaliah turns to the people and says, "You know, all that pious condemning that you are about to do . . . just remember, someday they'll hold it against you in Heaven," and he descends from the *bima.*

After meditating on the story for some time, this teaching came to the author on a sleepless night in the hours after learning her father had passed.

— N.M-Y., editor

I FIRST MET REB ELAZAR KENIG when I was a freshly minted *ba'alat t'shuvah,* still wet behind the ears and trying to find my way in the world. I knew that I needed to be a Ḥasid, and to be a Ḥasid you need to have a *rebbe.* So I had been praying for the guidance to find a *rebbe* that could nourish the appetite of my soul.

At the time, a friend of mine was living in S'fat; and while visiting her, we both went to pray in the Bratzlav Shul, where I heard Rav Kenig speak for the first time. Later, on *ḥol ha'moed Pesaḥ,* the two of us went with another friend to the Rav's house to speak directly with him. As soon as we walked through the door, I was overwhelmed by his presence. My soul swelled with the intensity of the moment and I struggled to hold back tears as I translated my friends' questions and the Rav's answers. Finally, it was my turn, and I asked the Rav how to learn Torah with my father without losing my footing on the path that I had chosen. The Rav answered, *"At yoda'at*—You know. You have the *da'at* (knowledge) that you need."

As I left his home, I could hardly see where I was going, my eyes were awash with a *mikvah* of tears. The Rav had touched my soul.

I needn't have been concerned that my father would try to alter my path. He was very proud of me, proud of my learning, proud of my children's learning, and had tremendous *naḥas* to be able to speak to me and my kids in Yiddish.

When I showed up for a visit in Boulder with my own electric burner, a pot and my own food, his wife Eve thought that I had lost my marbles and tried to convince me that their home was kosher. Abba just laughed and said that it serves him right. "When we were young in Ḥabad, we used to bless each other, 'May your kids be so *frum* that they won't eat in your home!' How could I be upset? The *b'rakhah* came true!"

My father was glad that I had become a Ḥasid of Reb Elazar Kenig and told me that he had known his father, Reb Gedaliah, and that he loved him very much.

I had heard from my father on another occasion that when he married my mother there were medical reasons that made it unclear if they would be able to have children. Along with the medical help that they sought out, they travelled to various *tzaddikim* and gurus to get *b'rakhot* to have children. In 1977, I was born.

It wasn't until many years later that I found pictures of Reb Gedaliah Kenig in my mother's picture albums. As far as I knew, there were only a handful of pictures of him in circulation, and I had found a gold mine. I had the pictures copied and brought them to my Rebbe, Reb Elazar Kenig, who was very grateful and deeply moved.

It was only later that I noticed that the pictures were taken when my parents had visited Israel in 1976. My father later confirmed that Reb Gedaliah was one of rebbes who had given them a *b'rakhah* to have children. So it is only fitting that his son is my *rebbe.*

This story of Reb Gedaliah teaching Rebbe Nahman is very touching. I take out of it a lesson that accompanies me throughout my life, my work, my parenting and my approach to the world. *Da'at*—use it to love and to connect.

Harsh judgment and the *da'at* of true connection are two opposites that cannot be held in one heart at the same time. It is not easy to always stay connected to our *da'at;* but it's our job, and it's worth the work. One cannot judge others harshly without it leaving some filthy residue on one's own mind, heart and tongue.

Da'at is not the kind of knowledge or understanding that will help you pass a test or remember the capital cities of all 50 states. It's about knowing that *Ha-Shem* is with you, loves you, and is guiding your steps. It allows you to show up for life, to be present and experience the interactions with everything that you've got. It doesn't mean that you'll always know what to do or say; but it helps you to be okay, even when you don't know.

My father used to talk about different classifications of Jews. Yes, there are those who consider themselves Reform Jews, Orthodox Jews, Post-denominational Jews, Non-reconformodox Jews, Under-constructionist Jews, and many other subdivisions to which people cling. Then you've got the Gastronomical Jews. They may not know from learning or *davvenen;* but when it comes to knishes, chulent and gefilte fish, they're Jewish 110% Jewish! It sounds like a joke, but it's actually a very deep thing. It's one thing to know *Ha-Shem* in your mind. It's another thing to know *Ha-Shem* in your heart. But to know *Ha-Shem* in your *kishkes* is really very deep.

My father once told me about a gathering that took place after Martin Buber's passing. Many scholars, rabbis and teachers were invited to speak, my father among them. Each one lectured about Martin Buber's teachings; but my father took a different approach. Instead of lecturing on the topic of 'I and Thou,' he asked the participants to divide up into pairs, turn their chairs towards each other, and take the time to experience the 'I-Thou' relationship in vivo, with eye contact and speech. In short, he invited them into a *"kishkes knowing"* experience.

True *da'at* is the deepest thing in the world. It is the greatest gift, one that generations of *tzaddikim* have striven to give to their students. Rebbe Nahman, in lesson seven of the second section of *Likkutei Maharan*, teaches that the real leaders of the Jewish people were those who had *rahamim*, or 'mercy' on their disciples. So what is true mercy? Giving people what they want is not always the greatest gift, because their desires may not be for their benefit, and may actually damage them. The greatest gift a *tzaddik* can give—true *rahamim*—is to give a person *da'at*, the ability to know *Ha-Shem*, themselves and others, the ability to connect on the deepest level. In my own language, the deepest gift is to help a person become not only a head-Jew, and not only a heart-Jew, but also a *kishkes*-Jew, and not merely in the gefilte fish sense.

Avraham Avinu was our father and teacher. He knew that to do true kindness, it isn't enough to merely talk to people about G-d; it's got to go below the belt. Feed them *matzah* and tongue in mustard. (In Boulder, that might be gluten free *matzah* and tofu with quinoa). In his own personal *avodah*, and for those of his disciples ready to go deeper, it meant *"brit milah, kishkes-*Judaism"—below the belt Judaism.

Moshe Rabbeinu led the people of Israel out of Egypt. He brought us to Sinai and we received the Torah. We said, *Na'aseh v'nishma*—"We will do and we will hear." The Midrash teaches that the angels tied two crowns to our heads; but that wasn't enough, because head-Judaism can't survive a real struggle. Only *"kishkes* Judaism"—real *da'at,* will get you through the rough and tumble patches of life. It took forty years of wandering in the desert until the *manna* had penetrated every molecule of our bodies, until we had built the *mishkan,* the tabernacle with our gold, sweat and struggle. Only then did we become *kishkes*-Jews, Jews with enough *da'at* to enter the Promised Land.

Enough talking about *da'at*. Here is an exercise to connect you to your own *da'at*. Please don't just read it and move on. Read it and stop for a minute, close your eyes and allow yourself to experience and digest it.

Picture yourself surrounded by some of the people who know you best—people who have seen you at your best and your worst, and who know the strength of your soul. Take a moment to look deeply into each person's eyes, one by one. As they look at you, they see not only your mind, not only your heart, they also see where your soul interfaces with your *kishkes.* In that place they know you, they love you, and they reflect back to you what they know about your ability to know and to connect in the deepest way. As you look into their eyes, they convey to you your own unique strengths, what makes you the only you in the galaxy— your soul-print. You are able to feel Ha-Shem's love for you as it is channeled through the love of those who surround you. Breathe deeply. Allow yourself to take it in. Breathe the love all the way down into your *kishkes.* Allow yourself to feel Ha-Shem's intent in your creation. Feel it strengthen and fortify you. Just stay there for a moment.

When you are surrounded and filled with love, your mind and soul can breathe and your *da'at* is nourished, allowing it to sit at the helm of your of your prefrontal cortex.

When you can feel your own *da'at* penetrating your molecules, go back to those who are with you. Look back into each person's eyes and tell them from your *kishkes* what you know about their own *da'at,* their soul-print, their unique gift. Take your time going around the circle.

When you are done, open your eyes. You will be ready to continue your day with *da'at.* You will be able to use your knowledge and discernment to find good in yourself and others, to live with *raḥamim,* and without the need to condemn others in order to define yourself. You will be able to be a *kishkes*-Jew.

My father did not choose any one successor. He wanted each and every one of us to succeed.

We each have our own unique gift, and have been given a mandate to use it for the benefit of ourselves, our families, our communities, and each other. I bless all of us to know our strengths, our unique soul-prints, and to have the *da'at,* the deep knowledge and connection to love ourselves and each other, and to live as walking, talking, eating, sleeping, living, knowing manifestations of *Ha-Shem* in this world.

I bless us all to be *kishkes*-Jews.

I know that's what Abba wanted.

APPENDIX A

Notes for a Lecture
by the Late Lubavitcher Rebbe

Translated by
ZALMAN SCHACHTER

I

HISTORICAL TIME as we know it could be divided into two periods. (A.) The period from the creation of the world until the giving of the Torah. (B.) The time since the giving of the Torah. The moment in which the Torah was given marks the appearence of the Jewish people. G-d adorned it by many words of praise, such as "Peculiar treasure, chosen people, and holy nation."

In the Torah we find these periods represented by *B'reshit,* the ancient days, and the giving of the Torah which begins after the Exodus. The tractate of *Avot,* in delineating the order of generations and their leaders, who with great devotion and self effacement brought the Torah's content to the chosen people, begins with the description of Moses receiving the Torah. "Moses receives the Torah from Sinai, transmitted it to Joshua, Joshua to the elders, the elders to the prophets, and the prophets passed it on to the men of the Great Assembly."

II

In Torah there is that which is apparent and that which is

hidden. Both the hidden and the apparent complement one another, although they are two separate things. We can observe people who are rooted in the apparent aspect of Torah. Such are not always aware of the hidden aspects of Torah, their very minds are closed to the inner Torah, and they are unable to grasp it. Although their minds are impermeable to the hidden aspects of Torah, they know the apparent aspects of Torah and observe its commandments in great detail and with the fear of Heaven. Yet their understanding and grasp is Golem-like, and crude. That their minds are closed to it, lies not G-d forbid in the area of faith or in the observance in commandments. The latter are taking great pains to observe the commands, be they of a positive, active nature, or of a negative avoidance nature. They observe the commandments at the proper time and are scrupulous in the observance of the negative commandments by being extremely careful not to do what ought not to be done.

Moreover, those with the impermeable minds are at times extreme in the details of the commandment, making fences that they may not, G-d forbid, stumble in the minute aspects of the commandment elaboration, etc. Nevertheless, all their observance is crude and automatic.

Anyone wishing to understand the reason for this crudity, as Ḥabad Hasidism sees it, will be able to do so by first understanding the difference between the position and the function of the limbs of the body.

The head and back side are both of greatest importance for man, yet it is easy to see how different they are in their quality and in their function.

III

This real difference between those of closed mind and those of the open mind is one that harks back yet to the beginning of creation. These two states are: (A.) The state from Adam to Abraham; and (B.) From Abraham on and further.

The time from creation until Abraham is darkness, and from

Abraham on there was light.

Thus it is stated that: "Until Abraham the world was lead in darkness, and from the time of Abraham on it began to be illuminated. Abraham began to radiate. The deeper meaning is that not only did Abraham himself live in light, but he began to give forth 'light,' with a completely committed and dedicated self-renouncing devotion to bring about the illumination of the darkness of the rest of the world. Ḥabad Hasidism explains that the work of Abraham, through the instrumentality of 'work' and observance of the commandments, as well as virtuous living, brought about in the transformation fo the very darkness itself, into light.

Adam, although he was created dust from the earth, the grossest of all the elements of fire, air, water and earth, was, on the other hand the creature of the very hands of G-d. "With his bodily radiance Adam darkened the light of the sun." Nevertheless, with all these marvelous qualities notwithstanding, Adam was a man of darkness.

Even Noah, whom the Torah terms *tzaddik*, perfectly righteous, was a *tzaddik* only when compared with the others in his generation. His righteousness was a self-centered one. Noah was not concerned to bring light to the lives of his contemporaries. Neither did he care enough to rouse in them a concern for knowing and caring, for the wider dissemination of the Divine. Abraham, on the other hand, was the first, who not only was concerned with bringing light into his own life, but also in spreading this light into the life of others. He sought to make G-d available to others. This is the meaning of the statement "From Abraham on it began to radiate."

IV

Abraham began to radiate, began to bring light into a materialistically dark world.

With deep devotion and self-effacement, dedication and sacrifice, he drew light into the world. He did this with the same virtues as had brought him to the readiness to offer his beloved son Isaac in conformance with the command of the Holy One, blessed be He.

Through this *M'sirat Nefesh* shown in the 'binding of Isaac,' a self-transcending loyalty beyond rationalizations or the rational, Abraham merited to fuse into his soul the power of bringing light to darkness.

The concept of 'light' can be taken on two levels. (1.) Light that can be seen; (2.) Light that lends itself to illumination. Not only is the latter stronger than the former, but also its strength is an inner one. External light, light that can be seen, has only the power to dazzle the beholder, but light which illumines creates light.

In the science and method of medical treatment, there are certain diseases in which the blood circulation in various members of the body has become weakened on account of an increase of fatty tissue. In such a case, light radiation is used for therapy. The light which is used medically is a weak sort of light; nevertheless, it penetrates deeply.

This is what we mean by Abraham beginning to illumine. Abraham was preceded by many righteous ones, some truly deserving of the name *tzaddik*. However, as far as the rest of the world was concerned, it has remained dark.

V

While it might seem superfluous to further elaborate this thought, we nevertheless might find that further structuring it will create a certain live intellectual flavor. This is due to the tapping of deeper and fresher sources of wisdom. As we all well know, Isaac and Jacob continued in their own way, to illuminate through this qualitative and essential light, which Abraham revealed and drew into 'containers.' These containers are none other but the children of Jacob. This simply means that the source of light, tapped by Abraham was continually drawn and channeled through Isaac, Jacob, and his children. This is further well explained in many books of 'apparent' Torah. Kabbalah and Hasidism further helped us to understand that although Jacob was already a monist [monotheist] working in 'lights,' as they are in 'vessels,' work in the order of *tikkun* universe, it was nevertheless still before the Torah was given.

Appendix B
The Geologist of the Soul

Zalman Schachter-Shalomi

Once, When I was still a Hillel director at the University of Manitoba in Winnipeg, I took a group of my students to meet my Rebbe, Rabbi Menachem Mendel Schneerson (1902-1994), the seventh Rebbe of Lubavitcher Rebbe. At that time, I served as the translator for them, translating into English from the Rebbe's Yiddish.

When the students got the opportunity to ask questions, one of them boldly asked the Rebbe, "What's a Rebbe good for?" I could have sunk through the floor in embarrassment; but the Rebbe wasn't offended at all and gave this wonderful answer:

"I can't speak about myself; but I can tell you about my own Rebbe. For me, my Rebbe was the geologist of the soul. You see, there are so many treasures in the earth. There is gold, there is silver, and there are diamonds. But if you don't know where to dig, you'll only find dirt and rocks and mud. The Rebbe can tell you where to dig, and what to dig for, but the digging you must do yourself."

Drawn from Zalman Schachter-Shalomi, *Geologist of the Soul: Talks on Rebbe-craft and Spiritual Leadership* (Boulder, CO: Albion-Andalus Books, 2012), xi.

Appendix C
a poetic remembering
for zalman

Carol Rose

invited to write a poem in honor of your ninetieth birthday beloved Zalman, i struggle to write a memorial reflection instead. i slip deeper into memory, recall that first glance, an RCMP beaver coat (complete with hugs) waiting at the Winnipeg airport to greet us, Shlomo & a seventeen year old enamored with your teachings, (on mimeographed sheets) a deep Torah translated for contemporary seekers. you were always a translator, Zalman, bringing the children of war-fractured parents & folks of different faiths closer ... & we, hungry for God, we learned the old texts (sweetened in your mouth) a Torah of poetry & song.

i remember that first Shabbos, your shtreimel, with tails that moved in a direction of their own, so like you, the essence Hasidic, the execution original ("a Picaso", i can hear you chuckle) & that twelve hour bus ride, in a snowstorm, crossing boarders, learning Kabbalah all night, using an overhead reading lamp to illustrate the breaking of vessels, *shevirat ha-keylim,* studying with you as Shlomo slept &, when you rested, learning with him, an immigration officer wondering at our entourage, two rabbis & a young woman.

but there is more, much more, the Sukkah at the Seminary on the eve of Aaron Ha-Cohen, a *tish* in Crown Heights, the Bobover in sky blue *kapota*, & me, waiting outside 770, alone ... the only woman in line ... waiting to get you *lekakh* from the Rebbe, Simchat Torah, you standing on top of a car on Eastern Parkway, leading us in song, *hevre* dancing in the streets until dawn.

our wedding & yours, a cheque for our rent, learning *gmilut hesed* (your actions always our greatest teacher) judaic studies, psychology of religion, dreaming of connecting basements (under separate houses buried in snow) Bnai Or/Pnai Or, "a community of left feet" you loved to call us, *Shabbos,* always *Shabbos,* your table or ours, guests from the House of Love & Prayer, chanting *Shalom Aleichem* to "Hail Hail the Gang's All Here," Purim at Hillel House ... Esther, Mordechai & Haman each with voices of their own, Pesah in Winnipeg & Philadelphia, Elijah's cup (in its many forms), your students, our friends, Art & TK, our children & yours, breaking the *sefer* barrier, birthing new ritual, sweetening the Psalms, a new *khap,* a new insight, dancing the Sefirotic map, becoming rainbows able to project multifaceted light, a paradigm shift, gender & identity becoming more permeable, the universe an organismic whole, finding ourselves on the growing edge, developing the heart muscle, loving & holding space for each other, the world, learning to *rebbe,* discovering the numinous ... together.

CONTRIBUTOR BIOGRAPHIES

RABBI BAHIR DAVIS is from a rabbinic family that includes his brother, father and grandfather, Rabbi Abraham Cronbach. He studied to become a rabbi at Hebrew Union College in New York and Israel, and has ordinations from both Rabbi Alexander Schindler and Rabbi Zalman Schachter-Shalomi. Reb Bahir is a maggid (storyteller) in the best tradition of Jewish storytelling, and is well-known for his vibrant humor and imagery. His eclectic background and study of Zen Buddhism, Aikido, Japanese and Native American culture all inform his approach to Judaism, and have opened up many insights on the nature of the Jewish path. He lives in Lafayette, Colorado, where he is the spiritual leader of Rocky Mountain Hai.

RABBI TIRZAH FIRESTONE is an author, psychotherapist, and the founding rabbi of Congregation Nevei Kodesh in Boulder, Colorado. A longtime student of Rabbi Zalman Schachter-Shalomi, she is widely known for her groundbreaking work on the re-integration of the feminine wisdom tradition within Judaism. Firestone lectures and teaches throughout the United States on spirituality, meditation, and the integration of ancient mystical wisdom into contemporary life. A leader in the international movement for the renewal of Judaism, she lives in Colorado with her husband David and their three children. She is the author of *With Roots In Heaven: One Woman's Passionate Journey into the Heart of Her Faith* (1998) and *The Receiving: Reclaiming Jewish Women's Wisdom* (2004).

PASTOR EMANUEL GOLDMANN, Ph.D., is a Protestant minister in Germany, and is presently serving as director of the Pastoral Seminary of the Evangelische Kirche von Kurhessen-Waldeck in Hofgeismar. A longtime student of Reb Zalman, Emanuel served as a minister in Jerusalem, and has been active in the field of Jewish-Christian ecumenism for many years. He is author of *Die grosse oekumenische Frage: Zur Strukturverschiedenheit christlicher und jüdischer Tradition mit ihrer Relevanz für die Begegnung der Kirche mit Israel* (1997).

RABBI LYNN GOTTLIEB is a feminist and the first woman ordained by Rabbi Zalman Schachter-Shalomi (and Rabbi Everett Gendler) in the Jewish Renewal Movement. She has served as a congregational rabbi at Temple Beth Or of the Deaf (1973-79), as spiritual leader and co-founder of Mishkan a Shul in New York City (1975-1980), as rabbi of Congregation Nahalat Shalom in Albuquerque, New Mexico (1981-2006), The Community of Living Traditions in Stony Point, New York, and Open Tent Shul of the Arts in Berkeley, California (2014 to present). She also co-founded Shomer Shalom Network for Jewish Nonviolence to advocate for non-violence as a core principle of Jewish life. Rabbi Gottlieb serves on the Rabbinic Council of Jewish Voice for Peace, and is a Freeman Fellow with The Fellowship of Reconciliation. Her recent books include: *Peace Primer II* and *Trail Guide for the Torah of Nonviolence.*

RABBI ARTHUR GREEN, PH.D., is one of the preeminent authorities on Jewish spirituality, mysticism, and Hasidism today. A student of Abraham Joshua Heschel, Nahum Glatzer, and Alexander Altmann, Green has taught Jewish mysticism, Hasidism, and theology to several generations of students at the University of Pennsylvania, the Reconstructionist Rabbinical College, Brandeis University, and Hebrew College, where he is currently Rector of the Rabbinical School. He first met Reb Zalman was he was a 16-year-old freshman at Brandeis University and remained a friend and colleague for the rest of his life. Some of his books include: *Tormented Master: Rabbi Nahman of Bratslav* (1980); *Your Word is Fire: The Hasidic Masters on Contemplative Prayer* (1993); *Ehyeh: A Kabbalah for Tomorrow* (2004); and *Radical Judaism: Rethinking God and Tradition* (2010); and *Speaking Torah: Spiritual Teachings Around the Maggid's Table* (2013). He lives in Newton, Massachusetts.

MAGGID MICHAEL L. KAGAN, Ph.D., is a teacher of Holistic Judaism (ordained as a sacred storyteller, teacher of Torah, and spiritual guide by Rabbi Zalman Schachter-Shalomi), as well as a scientist with a Ph.D. in Chemistry from Hebrew University. His Ph.D. thesis was essentially about the dynamics of paradigm shifts in chemical systems. He is the author of *The Holistic Haggadah* (2005), the editor of a collection of Reb Zalman prayer-translations, *All Breathing Life – At the Interface Between Poetry and Prayer* (2011), the author of *The King's Messenger: A Parable About Judaism* (2013), and *God's Prayer: A Sacred Challenge to Humanity* (2014). He lives in Israel with his wife Rabbi Ruth Gan Kagan, his five children and four grandchildren.

RABBI RUTH GAN KAGAN was born in Jerusalem. She grew up in a Zionist Orthodox family and is a descendent of a long line of Lithuanian Rabbis on her mother's side. She studied law at the Hebrew University and Torah at the Hartman and Pardes Institutes in Jerusalem. In the 1990s, she met Rabbi Zalman Schachter-Shalomi and later moved to Boulder, Colorado to study with him directly. In 2003, she was personally ordained by Reb Zalman and the ALEPH Rabbinic Program. In 2006, she published *Kirvat Elohim* (together with Reb Zalman), the first book in Modern Hebrew describing the principles and practice of Jewish Renewal. Today she is the spiritual leader of the Nava Tehila community in Jerusalem, which gives special emphasis to music and has produced two albums, *Dancing in the Glory* and *Waking Heart.*

RABBI LAURA DUHAN KAPLAN, Ph.D., is Director of the Iona-Pacific Inter-religious Center at the Vancouver School of Theology. Kaplan was ordained at ALEPH: Alliance for Jewish Renewal, and served for ten years as spiritual leader of Or Shalom Synagogue. She was formerly Professor and Chair of Philosophy at the University of North Carolina at Charlotte. For her innovative teaching of philosophy as a path to inner development, she was named United States Professor of the Year by the Carnegie Foundation for the Advancement of Teaching. She is the author of *Family Pictures: A Philosopher Explores the Familiar and Philosophy and Everyday Life* (1999).

RABBI MILES KRASSEN, PH.D., is one of the most authoratative teachers of Jewish meditation, Hasidism, and Kabbalah today, a teacher of comparative mysticism and the World's Wisdom Traditions, and a well-known musicologist. Having studied Kabbalah at the Hebrew University in Jerusalem and completed his doctorate in Hasidism at the University of Pennsylvania, he later received rabbinic ordination from Rabbi Zalman Schachter-Shalomi and the P'nai Or Religious Fellowship. Currently located in Albuquerque, NM, he serves as Rabbi of Planetary Judaism, an organization for disseminating progressive mystical Jewish teachings based on the spiritual insights of early Hasidism and Kabbalah. Some of his books include: *Isaiah Horowitz: The Generations of Adam* (1995); and *Uniter of Heaven and Earth: Rabbi Meshullam Feibush Heller of Zbarazh and the Rise of Hasidism in Eastern Galicia* (1998);

RABBI SHAUL MAGID, Ph.D., received his rabbinical ordination in Jerusalem in 1984, studied Jewish Thought at The Hebrew University from 1986-1989, and received his Ph.D. in Near Eastern and Jewish Studies at Brandeis in 1994. He was the Anna Smith Fine Assistant Professor of Jewish Studies at Rice University from 1994-1996. He joined the faculty at the Jewish Theological Seminary in 1996 where he was the chair of the Department of Jewish Philosophy until 2004. He presently holds the Jay and Jeannie Schottenstein Chair in Jewish Studies at Indiana University/Bloomington. Dr. Magid has published in the areas of Kabbalah, Hasidism, Modern Jewish Thought and contemporary American Judaism. He is the author of *Hasidism on the Margin: Reconciliation, Antinomianism, and Messianism in Izbica and Radzin Hasidism* (2003); *From Theosophy to Midrash: Myth, History and the Interpretation of Scripture in Lurianic Kabbalah* (2008); *American Post-Judaism: Identity and Renewal in a Postethnic Society* (2013); and *Hasidism Incarnate: Hasidism, Christianity, and the Construction of Modern Judaism* (2014). He is the editor of *God's Voice from the Void: Old and New Essays on Rabbi Nahman of Bratslav* (2003); and co-editor of *Beginning Again: Toward a Hermeneutic of Jewish Texts* (2004). He is also the rabbi of the Fire Island Synagogue in Sea View, NY.

PIR NETANEL (MU'IN AD-DIN) MILES-YÉPEZ, D.D., is the current head of the Inayati-Maimuni lineage of Sufism, co-founded with Zalman Schachter-Shalomi, fusing Sufi and Hasidic principles of spirituality and practice. He was born in Battle Creek, Michigan in 1972, and is descended from a Sefardi family of crypto-Jews. He studied History of Religions at Michigan State University and Contemplative Religion at Naropa University. He has been deeply involved in ecumenical dialogue and is considered a leading thinker in the InterSpiritual and New Monasticism movements. He is co-author (with Reb Zalman) of several works on Hasidic spirituality, *A Heart Afire: Stories and Teachings of the Early Hasidic Masters* (2009), *A Hidden Light: Stories and Teachings of Early HaBaD and Bratzlav Hasidism* (2011), *Foundations of the Fourth Turning of Hasidism: A Manifesto* (2014), and the editor of a new series of the works of Sufi master, Hazrat Inayat Khan. He currently teaches Contemplative Islam and Sufism in the Department of Religious Studies at Naropa University.

MATISYAHU MILLER, simply as Matisyahu to his fans, is a Grammy Award nominated singer-songwriter, known for his multi-influence fusion of hip-hop and reggae music with Hasidic-inspired lyrics. In 2001, he became a Ḥabad-Lubavitcher Ḥasid, having studied in the *ba'al t'shuvah yeshiva*, Hadar HaTorah, founded by Reb Zalman's own *mashpiyya*, Rabbi Yisroel Jacobson. In the Hasidic world, he found the key to unlock his own unique musical style. With the success of his second album, *Live at Stubb's* (2005), he was propelled into stardom as a "Hasidic reggae superstar." Though his early lyrics show the influence of Ḥabad-Lubavitch Hasidism, songs on his third album, *Youth* (2006) and especially his fourth album, *Light* (2009), are dominated by themes from Rebbe Nahman of Bratzlav. His fifth album, *Spark Seeker* (2012) is dedicated to the Ba'al Shem Tov and features samples of Reb Zalman on two tracks ("Bal Shem Tov" and "Searchin"). Today, he no longer identifies as a traditional Ḥasid of any lineage, but continues to be committed to Judaism and Hasidic spirituality. In 2014, he released his most personal album, *Akeda,* dealing with the struggles of 'the call' from God.

THOMAS ATUM O'KANE, Ph.D., is a senior Universalist Sufi teacher, and for thirty years a close personal student of Pir Vilayat Inayat-Khan. He is a graduate of the Guild for Spiritual Guidance, which focuses on the depth psychology of Carl Jung, the vision of Teilhard de Chardin and the practice of Christian Mysticism. He also holds a master's degree in Psychological Counseling and a doctorate in Transpersonal Psychology (Reb Zalman having served as his advisor for both). Today, O'Kane leads training programs in spiritual guidance in America, Canada and Europe for those in the helping professions, and leads various groups on spiritual pilgrimages.

RABBI NEHEMIA POLEN, Ph.D., is professor of Jewish thought and director of the Hasidic Text Institute at Hebrew College, Boston. He is the author of *The Holy Fire: The Teachings of Rabbi Kalonymus Shapira, The Rebbe of the Warsaw Ghetto (1999)*, winner of the 2002 National Jewish Book Award for *The Rebbe's Daughter: Memoir of a Hasidic Childhood* (2002) translated from the original Hebrew autobiography of Malkah Shapiro, and co-author with Laurence

Kushner of *Filling Words with Light* (2005).

CAROL ROSE was awarded the National Canadian Jewish Book Award for Poetry for her first collection of poems, *Behind the Blue Gate* (1997), and has recently published a second collection, *From the Dream* (2013). She is co-editor of the anthology, *Spider Woman: A Tapestry of Creativity and Healing* (1999). Carol and husband, Rabbi Dr. Neal Rose, were honored in Winnipeg in January 2015 with the Lieutenant Governor's Award for the Advancement of Interreligious Understanding from the Province of Manitoba. Information about her workshops can be obtained from rose@ ms.umanitoba.ca or mscarolrose.blogspot.com

RABBI NEAL ROSE, Ph.D., along with his wife Carol, was one of the founders of the original B'nai Or community in Winnipeg, Manitoba, and a professor in the Department of Judaic Studies (and later, Religious Studies) at the University of Manitoba from 1967-2000. From 2000-2013, he was the Director of Spiritual Care at the Simkin Center in Winnipeg. Currently, he is a Family Therapist in private practice and an inter-faith activist. Rabbi Rose and his wife Carol have five children and fourteen grandchildren.

SHALVI SCHACHTER WALDMAN, M.Sc., is a writer and psychotherapist working with women and couples in private practice in S'fat, Israel. She studied at the University of North Texas, Michlala Yerushalayim, and Neve Yerushalayim Family Institute. A Bratzlaver Hasid, Schachter has written numerous articles on Hasidic spirituality and Jewish religious life. She is the daughter of Rabbi Zalman Schachter-Shalomi, *z"l*.

RABBI DR. RAMI SHAPIRO, PH.D., is an award-winning author of over two-dozen books on religion and spirituality. He received rabbinical ordination from the Hebrew Union College–

Jewish Institute of Religion, and completed his doctorate at Union Graduate School. A congregational rabbi for 20 years, Shapiro currently co–directs One River Wisdom School (oneriverwisdomschool.com), blogs at rabbirami.blogspot.com, writes a regular column for Spirituality and Health magazine called "Roadside Assistance for the Spiritual Traveler," and hosts the weekly Internet radio show, How to be a Holy Rascal on Unity On-line Radio (www.unity.fm/program/howtobeaholyrascal). Some of his books include: *Minyan: Ten Principles for Living a Life of Integrity* (1997); *Hasidic Tales: Annotated & Explanined* (2010); and *Perennial Wisdom for the Spiritually Independent* (2013). He can be reached via his website, rabbirami.com.

Made in the USA
Columbia, SC
23 November 2020